American Anti-Pastoral

Ceres
RUTGERS
STUDIES
IN HISTORY

Ceres: Rutgers Studies in History

Lucia McMahon and Christopher T. Fisher,
Series Editors

New Jersey holds a unique place in the American story. One of the thirteen colonies in British North America and the original states of the United States, New Jersey plays a central, yet under-appreciated, place in America's economic, political, and social development. New Jersey's axial position as the nation's financial, intellectual, and political corridor has become something of a signature, evident in quips about the Turnpike and punchlines that end with its many exits. Yet, New Jersey is more than a cross-road or an interstitial "elsewhere." Far from being ancillary to the nation, New Jersey is an axis around which America's story has turned, and within its borders gather a rich collection of ideas, innovations, people, and politics. The region's historical develop-ment makes it a microcosm of the challenges and possibilities of the nation, and it also reflects the complexities of the modern, cosmopolitan world. Yet, far too little of the literature recognizes New Jersey's significance to the national story, and despite prom-ising scholarship done at the local level, New Jersey history often remains hidden in plain sight.

Ceres books represent new, rigorously peer-reviewed scholarship on New Jersey and the surrounding region. Named for the Roman goddess of prosperity portrayed on the New Jersey State Seal, Ceres provides a platform for cultivating and disseminat-ing the next generation of scholarship. It features the work of both established historians and a new generation of scholars across disciplines. Ceres aims to be field-shaping, providing a home for the newest and best empirical, archival, and theoreti-cal work on the region's past. We are also dedicated to fostering diverse and inclusive scholarship and hope to feature works addressing issues of social justice and activism.

For a complete list of titles in the series,
please see the last page of the book.

American Anti-Pastoral

• • • • • • • • • • • • • • • • • • • •

Brookside, New Jersey and the Garden State of Philip Roth

THOMAS GUSTAFSON

Rutgers University Press

New Brunswick, Camden, and Newark, New Jersey

London and Oxford

Rutgers University Press is a department of Rutgers, The State
University of New Jersey, one of the leading public research universities
in the nation. By publishing worldwide, it furthers the University's
mission of dedication to excellence in teaching, scholarship, research,
and clinical care.

Library of Congress Cataloging-in-Publication Data

Names: Gustafson, Thomas, 1953– author.
Title: American anti-pastoral : Brookside, New Jersey and the
    Garden State of Philip Roth / Thomas Gustafson.
Description: New Brunswick : Rutgers University Press, 2024. |
    Includes bibliographical references.
Identifiers: LCCN 2023046801 | ISBN 9781978838024 (paperback) |
    ISBN 9781978838031 (hardcover) | ISBN 9781978838048 (epub) |
    ISBN 9781978838055 (pdf)
Subjects: LCSH: Roth, Philip—Criticism and interpretation. |
    Roth, Philip. American pastoral. | New Jersey—In literature. |
    LCGFT: Literary criticism.
Classification: LCC PS3568.O855 Z686 2024 | DDC 813/.54—
    dc23/eng/20231222
LC record available at https://lccn.loc.gov/2023046801

A British Cataloging-in-Publication record for this book is available
from the British Library.

⊖ The paper used in this publication meets the requirements of the
American National Standard for Information Sciences—Permanence
of Paper for Printed Library Materials, ANSI Z39.48-1992.

rutgersuniversitypress.org

I've been drawn to depicting
the impact of place on
American lives.

—**PHILIP ROTH**, Interview

Contents

Illustrations

Abbreviations

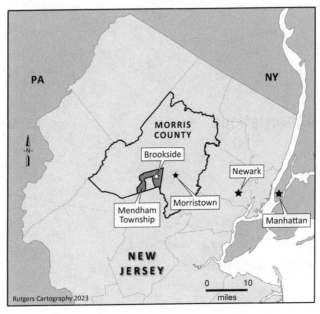

Map of northern New Jersey with Morris County, Mendham Township, and Brookside highlighted. Rutgers Cartography 2023, map by Michael Siegel.

American Anti-Pastoral

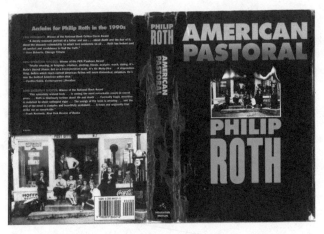

Original front and back cover of *American Pastoral* featuring the
Brookside post office, ringed in fire. 1997 hardcover first edition.
Jacket design by Milton Glaser, cover photograph by Matthew Klein.
(Author's collection.)

Prologue

● ● ● ● ● ● ● ● ● ●

William Carlos Williams, in his "Author's Note" for *Paterson*, begins: "*Paterson* is a long poem in four parts that a man in himself is a city, beginning, seeking, achieving and concluding his life in ways which the various aspects of a city may embody—if imaginatively conceived—any city, all the details of which may be made to voice his most intimate convictions."[1] This thesis of Williams about a man and a city could serve as a preface to Philip Roth's *American Pastoral*. Roth himself gives a variation of it in a comment he made in an interview: "I've been drawn to depicting the impact of place on American lives."[2] This book is about the imaginary Old Rimrock of Roth's novel and Brookside, the direct model for Roth's Old Rimrock, and how these places figure in the lives of a range of people imaginary and real who have had an intimate association with the place for one reason or another: Philip Roth and his characters Swede Levov, Bill Orcutt, Bucky Robinson; George Washington, Chris Christie, Whitney Houston; the poets Christopher Merrill and Steven Cramer; the historian John T. Cunningham; Joachim Prinz; and Swede's daughter, Merry, who, in an act of protest against the

Vietnam War, blows up with a bomb the post office in the center of the town of Old Rimrock.

Philip Roth is now one of three contemporary writers to have his complete works published by the Library of America. Literary criticism of Roth recognizes his American trilogy to be at the heart of his body of work, and the primary thrust of scholarship on Roth's American trilogy conforms to what one of Roth's best readers—Michael Kimmage—argues in his *In History's Grip: Philip Roth's Newark Trilogy*: Roth's literary scrutiny of Newark is not just a scrutiny of Newark but of America itself as Roth makes Newark a "vehicle for exploring American character in conjunction with American history, the intersection of character and history on a national scale, running from the 1930s to the 1990s."[3] What this book emphasizes is that Roth uses Old Rimrock as he uses Newark: he makes a scrutiny of Old Rimrock and Morristown and its Revolutionary era history a vehicle for studying the conflicts of America in the 1960s as well as the conflicts and desires that have been so much part of the American experience since its first colonization: the desire to escape the past, the desire for a place free from the burdens of class and ethnic discrimination, the desire for a place of exodus that would be a source of re-genesis: "a fresh, green breast of the new world," as invoked by F. Scott Fitzgerald at the end of *The Great Gatsby*.[4] Since the beginning of his literary career with *Goodbye, Columbus*, Roth's fictions set in Newark have always been in an engaged relationship with the New Jersey outside of Newark, and this is certainly the case of *American Pastoral*. But the history of places in New Jersey outside of Newark and their relationship to characters such as Swede Levov has been more difficult to access independently from Roth's storytelling, so an Old Rimrock is left as one scholar calls it a "mythic rural paradise."[5] Trust me, Old Rimrock is no less mythical than Roth's Newark.

On the front cover of the first edition of *American Pastoral* is a picture of the Brookside post office that I walked by almost every day for nine years on the way to my K–8 elementary school and where I or a member of my family picked up our mail each day from a box inside it. This book is a hybrid of a critical study of Roth's *American Pastoral*, a history of Brookside, and a cultural reflection about New Jersey literature and the pastoral vision of America in one of its strongest variations: the dream of a new Eden, the dream of a chosen land where we can regain our freedom, the dream of creating and preserving for our pursuit of happiness a home, a model community, a city on a hill, a place that would be in harmony with nature and with people in harmony with each other. Roth makes of Old Rimrock for Swede such a place, an idyllic town in the highlands of western Morris County: a green garden in a green shade in the Garden State. But then Merry's bombing of its post office and the verbal bombs thrown at the town by Swede's brother and father, Jerry and Lou, rip the fig leaves off this pastoral world, an uncovering furthered by Bucky Robinson's revelations about the history of antisemitism in Morris County. This study seeks to extend this counter-pastoral critique of Swede's Arcadian vision of Old Rimrock, an effort that has its roots in my coming of age in Brookside during the 1960s, one year younger than Merry Levov, and discovering, while researching the history of the zoning laws of my town for a college seminar entitled Public Policymaking Affecting Land Use in fall 1974, the unspoken origins of that regulation in the

1930s in part as an effort to prevent the spread of a largely Jewish town, Mt. Freedom, and its summer bungalow colonies, into neighboring Brookside.

William Carlos Williams describes the four parts of *Paterson* in his "Author's Note" as follows: "Part One introduces the elemental character of the place. The Second Part comprises the modern replicas. Three will seek a language to make them vocal, and Four, the river below the falls, will be reminiscent of episodes—all that any one man may achieve in a lifetime."[6] Roth structures *American Pastoral* into a trinity that makes it something of an inverted *Divine Comedy*: part I is "Paradise Remembered," part II, "The Fall," and part III, "Paradise Lost." The three parts of my study echo this structure and the structure of *Paterson*. Part I, Dismal Harmony, named after a place with a stream and falls near the center of Brookside, introduces the elemental character of Old Rimrock for Swede Levov and a short history of Brookside including a Vietnam War protest in 1969 at its celebrated Fourth of July parade. Part II, Babel, takes us deeper into the history of this place through tours of its past given in the novel by the WASP, Bill Orcutt, the Jew, Bucky Robinson, and the dissonant voices of Lou and Jerry Levov as well as through a portrait of the civil rights activism in Morristown of Beatrice Jenkins. Part III gives us Old Rimrock after the fall for Swede and Brookside after the 1960s from the perspective of its history and environmental politics and NIMBY activism: the efforts to wall off its garden and protect its greenness.

Williams cites John Dewey in his "Author's Note": "The local is the only universal, upon that all art builds."[7] *Paterson* and *American Pastoral* both are built on that premise, as is so much of the literature of New Jersey. But I argue in my epilogue that what makes *American Pastoral* more "universal" as a work of art—and arguably the best novel of New Jersey—is that it builds fundamentally on not one but two contrasting localities—the Essex County of Newark and Elizabeth, on the one hand, and the Morris County of Brookside and Morristown on the other—and on the history of each going back to that other era of revolution in America long before the late 1960s: the time when George Washington and his Continental army encamped for two winters in Morristown and Jockey Hollow and fought more of its battles in New Jersey than any other state. Through literary allusion and invocation of myth, both biblical and American, and through its historical as well as geographic setting, Roth also makes an infamously peripheral place—New Jersey—the home of this great American novel. New Jersey is infamous for feeling peripheral to New York, and western Morris County has too often been peripheral to a New Jersey imagined as centered up and down the New Jersey Turnpike (the territory of Walt Whitman, William Carlos Williams, Allen Ginsberg, and Janet Evanovich) or down along the southern part served by exits off the Garden State Parkway (the territory of Robert Pinsky and Bruce Springsteen). Brookside itself feels peripheral to Morristown as the town is mostly unknown to the people living in this county seat just five miles away. It is thus a place triply outcast: peripheral to Morristown, which is peripheral to a northern New Jersey centered in Bergen, Essex, and Union counties, which is peripheral to New York City. Yet Brookside is a place not of outcasts, but insiders—people on the inside of power and privilege gained from wealth, inherited and achieved. For instance, it is now the home of former Governor Chris Christie, whose first elected position was as a freeholder for Morris County.

There is in America the story of the invisibility of Blackness and of people low in power; there is also in America the story of the invisibility of those hidden on high and the ways their power operates. This book is my attempt to make this power, so marked by whiteness, more visible, more down to earth, more familiar, indeed more in the family (as my father and mother both served Mendham Township, the municipality of Brookside, as elected officials) and reveal how it hides so often in the underground roots of green power or behind that fig leaf of a euphemism: protecting the environment. The green world of Old Rimrock—and its whiteness—seem so far removed from Newark and its Blackness. On the one hand, there is the New Jersey of Newark and Elizabeth close to an exit off the Turnpike that is reputedly a city of ashes world near a toxic dump. But there is also still in the Garden State of New Jersey the green world that is Brookside, a paradise for some that has not been lost of nice homes with a nice yard in a village almost on a hill amid woods with a main street and streams running through it, and it seems never the twain shall meet. But Roth, in his artistic vision, brings them in a close relationship (as did the Mt. Laurel decision in its vision of justice): there is something natural about the greenness of Brookside, but not its current 85 percent whiteness.[8] Even the continuing greenness of Brookside—and the growth of that greenness through the purchase and protection of more park land—is a consequence, like its whiteness, of the operations of law, power, and privilege. Indeed, the worlds of Brookside and Newark are no more separate from each other than the origins and consequences of Brookside's implicit efforts through zoning to protect itself from becoming as Jewish as Mt. Freedom, as Black as Morristown, and as Latino as Dover. The history of America, the history of New Jersey, the history of Brookside—like the stories of Philip Roth's Garden State—are a story of exclusion juxtaposed against a dream and a struggle to be more inclusive.

American Pastoral first mentions Old Rimrock in a quick allusion not far from the opening of the novel, when Nathan Zuckerman, the narrator of the story, describes Swede commuting to his business on Central Avenue in Newark "from his home some thirty-odd miles west of Newark, out past the suburbs—a short-range pioneer living on a hundred-acre farm on a back road in the sparsely habitated hills beyond Morristown, in wealthy, rural Old Rimrock, New Jersey" (AP, p. 14). Shortly thereafter, in the second allusion, Zuckerman imagines golfers in Old Rimrock, after a round of golf, trooping back to the clubhouse as Ivan Ilyches saying to themselves, "It doesn't get any better than this" (p. 31). The Mendham Golf & Tennis club, whose territory is in Mendham Township and adjacent to Mendham Borough, was founded as a nine-hole private course off Kennaday Road in 1961 in part to protect the land from being sold off for residential development. It was expanded in 1969 into an eighteen-hole course, stretching across the other side of Corey Lane, not more than a mile south on this same street where former Governor Chris Christie now lives. Membership in this club was a sign of prestige, and one of the most exclusive housing developments in the town is a development of five-acre zoned lots mostly in a wooded area that surrounds several holes of this course.[9]

I had a classmate in elementary school whose family moved from the South to Brookside and a home on Hilltop Circle Road after his father was transferred from the Bell Labs in North Carolina to the Bell Labs in Murray

Hill, New Jersey. His parents were refused membership in the golf club. They did not fit in, it seems. All three of their kids—an older daughter, and two sons—had troubles "fitting in," particularly the older daughter, who I remember being told attempted suicide or committed it in her late teenage or young adult years. Their mother, my mom told me when I was a bit older, was an alcoholic. The family had one other trouble. Their youngest son had two fingers on a hand mangled when they got caught in an open conveyor belt for bringing up packages from a basement storage area in the local grocery store, the Foodtown in Mendham Borough. But what I remember so clearly about this family was my classmate telling me how angry his father was for being rejected at the golf club where I also remember, so clearly and beautifully, how wonderful it was, as a family, to play there on summer evenings as a foursome: my father, my mother, my brother, and me. On Sundays in the spring and summer my mom would sometimes take us to church. My father would usually play golf and then work out in the garden on Sundays, never taking up my mom's urging to join us at church, saying, "I can see more of God on the golf course and in the garden than people can see in church." That is the American pastoral spirit for me. This is Emerson and Thoreau and William Cullen Bryant for me. But this pastoral world of the golf course where I can hear my father saying on a summer evening there, "It doesn't get any better than this," was an unhappy, even reprehensible, place of rejection for my classmate's family.

This anecdote of this family's rejection from the garden world of the Mendham Golf & Tennis Club and my memories of their kids not fitting in quite right in Brookside is to me the other side of the American pastoral that affects my reading of Roth's novel and recalls for me in a much milder form the expulsions from the new Eden or community club world—the city on a hill—that the patriarchs of the Puritan world (John Winthrop, John Endicott, William Bradford, and so on) were trying to re-create. Infamously, these patriarchs exiled Roger Williams and Anne Hutchinson, who did not fit it, and they perpetrated the destruction of Thomas Morton's Merrymount and the Pequot village in Mystic, Connecticut, where 400 Pequot Indians were surrounded and fired upon and burned in 1630, an act for which the Puritans gave thanks to God. The narrator of Philip Roth's *Dying Animal* sides with the outcast Thomas Morton and wonders about the cultural direction America might have taken if Morton's Merrymount, not Bradford's Plymouth, had been the winner. This is a study of the insiders and outsiders of Brookside and Roth's Old Rimrock and how Roth in *America Pastoral* takes us so deeply inside the conflicts of American history and culture in this place.

Part I

Dismal Harmony

● ● ● ● ● ● ● ● ● ●

1. The Office of Letters and the Bomb: Brookside and Old Rimrock

Brookside, at its center, is simply a post office, a municipal building, a community club, a baseball field, a church, and brooks wending through it. It is just five miles from Morristown, but most people in Morristown have never heard of it. The town is part of Mendham Township, which consists of several neighborhoods—in particular, Brookside, Ralston, and Washington Valley—with an old schoolhouse the main feature of Washington Valley, a general store (now a museum) the main feature of Ralston, and the post office dating back to 1879 the main feature of Brookside, which is the government center for Mendham Township. What distinguishes in part the boundary of Brookside is the zip code—07926—and that there is no delivery of mail: Brooksiders pick up their mail from the post office. A picture of the post office with teenagers gathered on the steps, which includes the mother of my best friend growing up, is on the front and back cover of the first edition of Roth's *American Pastoral*. In the novel, the

11

daughter of Swede Levov, in an act of protest against the Vietnam War in 1968, blows up a combination of post office and general store with a bomb in the early morning, which kills a resident, Dr. Conlon, picking up his mail. Roth gets the history almost right: solely a post office in 1968, this building had once been a general store doubled with a post office inside of it, and it had "served the old farming community as its meeting place since the days of Warren Gamaliel Harding. . . . A meeting place, a greeting place" (AP, p. 317). But maybe even more than Roth could imagine it, Merry strikes at the heart of the community. Brookside, like every polis, is a creation of talk, of communion through the word, the sharing of stories, gossip, or just quick hellos, and there was no place in that town— not the church, the Community Club, the school, nor the baseball field—that could rival that post office as a forum for the exchange of talk, with all its chances for greetings of good will, the bonhomie of Brookside.[1]

The bombing by Merry—she becomes infamous as the "Old Rimrock Bomber"—leads Nathan Zuckerman, the narrator of *American Pastoral*, to reflect: "History, American history, the stuff you read about in books and study in school, had made its way out to tranquil, untrafficked Old Rimrock, New Jersey, to countryside where it had not put in an appearance that was notable since Washington's army twice wintered in the highlands adjacent to Morristown" (p. 87). Roth makes no mention in any of his published writings that Old Rimrock is based on Brookside, but here in the novel is the first clue, confirmed indubitably by lines that come nearly one hundred pages later: "Basically the village is one street. Going east there is the new Presbyterian church. . . . Diagonally across from where the store used to be is the yellow stuccoed six-room schoolhouse" (p. 167). Washington had his headquarters in a mansion in nearby Morristown that was de rigueur for school field trips—Swede Levov visited the state park with his fourth-grade class—and Washington's army had its encampment in Jockey Hollow, which is partly in Mendham Township where replicas of the soldier huts can be visited. Creating a Revolutionary war context for Merry's bombing, the novel continues, "History, which had made no drastic impingement on the daily life of the local populace since the Revolutionary War, wended its way back out to these cloistered hills and, improbably, with all its predictable unforeseenness, broke helter-skelter into the orderly household of the Seymour Levovs and left the place in a shambles. People think of history in the long term, but history, in fact, is a very sudden thing" (p. 87). Suddenly, it is not an act of history in the context of this fiction that shocks me, but an act of literature itself—a Pulitzer Prize–winning novel—that comes out to Brookside and makes this untrafficked place the local habitation and name for the American pastoral, that vision of the "fresh, green breast of the new world" summoned up time again as if in prayer by Jefferson, Cooper, Emerson, Thoreau, Twain, Fitzgerald, Faulkner, Hurston and so on.[2] After Merry's bombing, a young man, Edgar Bartley, who had a date to the movies in Morristown with Merry, is quoted in an editorial in the local newspaper on the bombing as saying, "I always thought of Old Rimrock as a place where nothing can happen to you" (p. 169). I thought that too at Edgar's age. But Roth blows that up big time. America happens here for the Levovs. America—in its literature and culture and politics—happens here now as Roth makes this place the home of a conflict at the heart of our history: a conflict between the office of the letter and the bomb, the word and violence, and the principle of equality and the practice of exclusion in American democracy.

2. Fourth of July Parade

The Brookside Community Club has hosted for the town since 1923 along East Main Street a Fourth of July parade that it calls "The Grandest Little Parade in America."[1] The township had five minutes of fame attached to it as the place where Whitney Houston settled and married Bobby Brown, and it might have had another fifteen minutes as the home of former Governor Chris Christie if he had won the Republican nomination for the presidency in 2016. More remarkably for me, this town is the location of three works of literature, one renowned (*American Pastoral*) and two minor works, each of which revolves in part around a lyrical memory of an anti-war protest. Two poets from Brookside, Christopher Merrill and Steven Cramer (both near the age of Merry Levov in 1968), have written poems about a Vietnam War protest staged by high school students in the midst of the Fourth of July parade in 1969. The protestors carried a coffin at the end of this parade representing people dead to the horrors of the war and the responsibilities of democracy, then refused to stand for the Pledge of Allegiance and the playing of "The Star-Spangled Banner" at the opening ceremonies. This refusal prompted Sam Tufts, a leader of the volunteer fire department, a coach of many of Brookside's baseball teams, and later the mayor of the town, to lift a protestor roughly and make him stand for the anthem, an act prompted not just by his patriotism but by the fact that his nephew, Robert Bruce Tufts, was

Dismal Harmony • 15

Brookside Fourth of July Parade protest, 1969. *Observer-Tribune* newspaper, July 17, 1969, p. 12. (Courtesy of Ken Lurie.)

killed by a land mine while serving in the Vietnam War just three weeks earlier. Christopher Merrill's poem, "The Parade: July 4th, 1970," describes "nine young men, dressed in black robes" carrying an "empty coffin on their shoulders" who were met with silence from porches that then "Crackled" after they passed.[2] Steven Cramer's poem, "The Parade, 1968," describes the "Gustafsons, / The Gibbs, the Tufts" jeering at the protest and mailing (allegedly) the mothers of the protestors "envelopes / Of dung."[3] This historical act of protest by students during the parade mirrors in some deeply resonant ways the key action of Roth's novel, wherein the daughter of Swede Levov blows up the post office in the center of the town with a bomb in her own act of anti-war protest.

Merry Levov's bombing reminds us that violence, as H. Rap Brown said, is as American as cherry pie and the beginning of the United States in a revolution declared on July 4, 1776. We can hear that violence in Jimi Hendrix's 1969 rendition at Woodstock of "The Star-Spangled Banner," the national anthem the Brookside protestors refused to honor in 1969. President Ronald Reagan in his second inaugural address claims the "American sound" is "hopeful, big-hearted, idealistic—daring, decent and fair."[4] Hendrix's magnificent rendition of "The Star-Spangled Banner," one of the greatest works of art to emerge from the era of Vietnam War protest, brings into that song all the cacophonous sounds of war and violence that were the frazzle of dissonance of America in the late 1960s. As Tony Kushner argues in his essay, "American Things," the frazzle of dissonance can be dangerous—it is the riot of the unheard that rocked Roth's Newark in 1967 and Merry Levov's protest bomb that kills Dr. Conlon.[5] But it can also be part of the movement forward, as Thomas Paine preached and practiced long before the 1960s. An embrace of the harmonious can also be dangerous. It can stifle the frazzle of freedom. It can hide injustice under a fig leaf to protect the pastoral. The desire for the peaceful green breast of a new world can take us backward in nostalgia: an escape from Babel to an imagined garden state that is as real as Jay Gatsby.

What Steven Cramer and his friends did in their Vietnam War protest in Brookside is not dissimilar to what Merry Levov does in bombing the Old Rimrock post office, except for one very palpable difference: her protest is violent, and it becomes deadly when it kills Dr. Conlon. Merry's act of protest is also not dissimilar from the "shot heard round the world" at Lexington and

Concord and the declaration of war on July 4, 1776, when Thomas Jefferson's draft of the Declaration of Independence was approved by the Continental Congress (after the editing out of its tortured defense of "the sacred rights and liberties" of African peoples).[6] Its justification of violence led to the creation of the United States and to its commemoration in Brookside's Fourth of July parade. One of our family floats in the Fourth of July parade in 1957 re-enacted Molly Pitcher's actions at the Battle of Monmouth. My sister, standing by a well with a bucket, was Molly, and my older brother and I, dressed in tricorne hats, were Continental army soldiers, my brother bearing a musket while I am packing a colonial pistol in my waistband. In another Fourth of July parade, a year earlier, at the age of three, I was a cowboy riding my rocking horse in a red wagon pulled by my father and sporting a toy rifle with my stuffed animals strung up as trophies of "A Good Day's Hunting." What is so manifest in these family floats for the Fourth of July parade—and what should be made manifest in any study of American politics (as Richard Slotkin has taught us in his trilogy of books on the myth of the frontier and American regeneration through violence)—is the power of the gun. We are, in Jill Lepore's words, "One Nation, Under the Gun," the subtitle of an essay she wrote for the *New Yorker* called "Battleground America."[7] The Revolutionary War competes for our most mythologized and declawed war: the talons of its violence as a civil war are hidden or turned into parade celebrations that cover up America in its foundational violence and afterward in its eagle of empire predation.

A statue of Thomas Paine in Morristown in Burnham Park is one of the first things one passes traveling from Brookside into Morristown along Route 24. Dedicated on

Fourth of July float, 1957. Gustafson children re-enacting Molly Pitcher and the Battle of Monmouth. (Author's collection.)

Statue of Thomas Paine in Burnham Park, Morristown, New Jersey, by Georg John Lober, 1950. (Photo by Dianne L. Durante, 2019.)

July 4, 1950, the statue has Paine, seated, with a long musket across his lap, writing with a quill pen. Citations from his most famous works are inscribed on the walls that form the base of the statue. One of its inscriptions reads: "Washington's sword would have been wielded in vain had it not been supported by the pen of Paine." The statue incarnates the saying, "The Pen is Mightier than the Sword."[8] The iconography of Paine's statue blinds us, however, to the degree that the gun, not the word, won the Revolution. Our mythology of the Revolution obscures what Nathaniel Hawthorne reveals in his literary deconstruction of mythology about colonial protest in his story "My

Kinsman, Major Molineux." In the story, a mob, led by a man with a face "blazed" half in "intense red" ("an emblem of fire and sword") and half "black as midnight" (betokening "the mourning which attends them")—"a fiend of fire and a fiend of darkness"—with a train following him of "wild figures in the Indian dress"—a potent symbol of the "indigenous American berserk" as Philip Roth terms it (AP, p. 86)—go about, in "counterfeited pomp, in senseless uproar, in frenzied merriment, trampling all on an old man's heart."[9] The narrative voice of this story, like the voice of Nathan Zuckerman and Swede Levov, seems appalled at this eruption of the "indigenous American berserk," which tramples on the heart of Major Molineux as much as Merry Levov's bombing tramples on the heart of Swede Levov and devastates the mind of his wife, Dawn Dwyer, a former Miss New Jersey, who suffers bouts of depression and emotional breakdown in the wake of Merry's bombing. But this "indigenous American berserk" is, of course, the "berserk" of the Boston Tea Party, when colonists in Boston dressed as Indians dumped into the harbor 340 chests of tea (worth today an estimated $1,700,000) in protest against a new tax on tea, and the "berserk" of colonists erupting in protest against the Stamp Act in 1765 by mobbing effigies of English officials and looting and marauding the home of Thomas Hutchinson, lieutenant governor of Massachusetts, for his support of it. Just as Hawthorne cautions us against sentimentalizing colonial protest in "My Kinsman, Major Molineux," so too does Roth caution us against pastoralizing the protests against the Vietnam War. But there is a danger too in locating an innocent time and place in Old Rimrock.

3. Indigenous American Berserk

Merry Levov is characterized by Nathan Zuckerman as "the angry, rebarbative spitting-out daughter with no interest whatever in being the next successful Levov" (p. 86). Instead, this daughter—and the late 1960s—are claimed to blast "to smithereens" her father's "particular form of utopian thinking" and bring into "Swede's castle"—his stone house in Old Rimrock—a "plague" (p. 86). Zuckerman continues to describe Merry as the "daughter who transports him out of the longed-for American pastoral and into everything that is its antithesis and its enemy, into the fury, the violence, and the desperation of the counterpastoral—into the indigenous American berserk" (p. 86). The Puritan fathers in New England began to lament not too long after their exodus from the old world how their sons and daughters were betraying their errand into the wilderness and its dream to create a model of Christian charity, as this younger generation pursued instead the pleasures and profits that John Winthrop warned against embracing at the end of his lay sermon—known now as his City on a Hill address—delivered in 1630 aboard the *Arbella*. Thomas Morton and his band of revelers at Merrymount had gone native enough, consorting in their own "berserkness" with the Indigenous peoples of America. Morton himself is described by another novelist Roth creates, David Kepesh in *The Dying Animal*, as a "forest creature" and "merry miscegenator" and a "colonial harbinger" of the "national upheaval" of "the sixties" that makes this decade not "aberrant" but a flowering of a New England tradition of "personal freedom" and "no-rules" with Morton our "founding father."[1] But it is the "Sons of Liberty" in colonial New England who would embrace most fervently—with fury and desperation and violence—an anti-patriarchal politics of liberation, rebelling against their parent country, England, and their putative father, King George III, animated by the counter-Court and counter-corruption politics of classical republicanism that had much the same fury and "berserkness" to it that marks Merry's opposition to Lyndon B. Johnson (LBJ) and the Vietnam War.

The "shot heard round the world"—the first act of violence that marks the beginning of the Revolutionary War—was fired in Massachusetts. No Ralph Waldo Emerson and no Henry Wadsworth Longfellow have composed poems to honor the actions of the Revolutionary War in New Jersey, but more than Massachusetts, this state is the home of the significant turning-point battles of the American Revolution, including the battles of Trenton, Monmouth, Princeton, and Springfield. Morristown itself, where Merry Levov attends high school, calls itself the "military capital of the American Revolution," and the school mascot is the Colonials—the name too of a Brookside Little League team I played for—and the school mascot for West Morris Mendham High School, established in 1970, is the Minutemen.[2] In 1777, after victories at Trenton and Princeton, General Washington and the Continental army marched to the Morristown area where Washington made an encampment and where he lived in Jacob Arnold's tavern located on the Morristown Green. Washington and the Continental army had its second encampment in Morristown from December 1779 to June 1780, with his troops stationed at Jockey Hollow, located along the edge of Morris Township and Mendham

Township. Washington's own headquarters this time was the Ford Mansion. The headquarters are now part of Morristown National Historical Park, dedicated in 1936, and the first such national historical park in the country. Swede Levov's fourth-grade class comes out from Newark to visit it, as did classes at Mendham Township Elementary School.

If the American Revolution can be seen as an eruption of an "indigenous American berserk" that makes violence as American as cherry pie, then Merry Levov's bombing is another serving of the pie.[3] Violence—and symbolic acts of violence—are as much a part of myth and history in America as Johnny Appleseed. The sword and the gun rival—if not surpass—the ax and plow as icons of America's expansion by conquest of the wilderness, the green world that was, in the beginning, the land of Indigenous people (the Lenape in Morris County, New Jersey). Merry's violence, her bombing of the post office in Old Rimrock, thus does not fall far from the tree: The center of Old Rimrock is seven miles from Washington's Headquarters, 4.5 miles from a statue of Thomas Paine in Burnham Park, 4.5 miles from Jockey Hollow, and eight miles from the iron mines of Ironia and Mine Hill that made this part of New Jersey a center of the military-industrial complex for the American Revolution.[4] Washington chose Morristown as the location for his headquarters and an encampment of the Continental army not just because of its strategic location between New York City and Philadelphia (and the natural barricade of the Watchung Mountains and Great Swamp) but also because the area had the natural resources, local industries, and skilled workers to provide the arms to support the army as well as the farmland to feed it. The berserk of Merry is, in a word, as indigenous to this area as cows and the cultivation of peaches, with the Revolutionary battlefields of New Jersey as much a flipside to the farming of the Garden State as Merry is the flipside to the Swede, her father, as a Johnny Appleseed, and to Dawn, her mother, as a cattle breeder. The American Revolution itself was not just a tax revolt; it was led by colonists with a paranoid fear that England was conspiring against its liberties and by ministers and pamphleteers who called for a holy crusade against an evil empire including one man with a statue in Morristown—Thomas Paine—who would later call for the redistribution of wealth through taxation to provide forms of social security for the elderly and the poor and financial grants to the newly married and new parents.[5] (Now how berserk is that?)

Philip Roth creates the world of the American pastoral—the suburban world of the garden state of New Jersey—as a refuge for Swede Levov from the berserk of Newark and its riots. In Brookside, the volunteer fire department was ready to deputize itself during the Newark riots in 1967 to defend Brookside from rioters. Berkeley, California came to be known as "Berserkeley" in the 1960s as it became the *locus contemporaneous* for America's "indigenous American berserk," a "berserk" that broke out in protest in the Arcadian world of California in the mid-1960s the same way that Seymour Levov's daughter breaks out in protest of the Vietnam War in Old Rimrock by bombing the post office. In the late 1960s, the "indigenous American berserk" was taking over administration buildings at Berkeley and Columbia and occupying the student union at Cornell and taking over Alcatraz and people of color and women were breaking into bastions of white male power thanks to the civil rights and the feminist movements. In Brookside, it took over the Fourth of July parade. Some of the participants in this protest had participated a short time before in June in an all-night peace vigil on the Morristown Green, keeping company with its memorials and statues to the Revolutionary War and the Civil War. In 1970, over the Labor Day holiday, Vietnam Veterans Against the War began one of their first major protests on the Morristown Green, marching from this capital of the Revolution to Valley Forge, staging along the way mock search-and-destroy actions in White House Station, New Jersey and other local communities in which they enacted scenes of soldiers mistreating Vietnamese civilians in village sweeps, a protest that was met by jeers and dismissal from citizens in this rural part of western New Jersey.[6]

In a 1981 interview, Philip Roth declares, when asked to "assess the sixties" and decide whether it was a "decade of liberation" or an "era of arrogance, of narrow new dogmas": "I have no judgment to make of something so colossal as ten years of world history" (RMO, p. 103). He adds, "As an American citizen I was appalled and mortified by the war in Vietnam, frightened by the urban violence, sickened by the assassinations, confused by the student uprisings, sympathetic to the libertarian pressure groups, delighted by the pervasive theatricality, disheartened by the rhetoric of the causes, excited by the sexual display, and enlivened by the general air of confrontation and change" (RMO, p. 103). Twenty years after this interview, in writing *American Pastoral*, Roth seems to forget his hesitation to make a judgment of "something so colossal as ten years of world history" as this novel does much to ventriloquize through its babel of voices the positions Roth takes in each clause of his following sentence. But in *American*

Pastoral, Roth does not forget what appalled and mortified him about the Vietnam War. Nor is he any less stringent than George Orwell—or the voice of his novel *Our Gang*—against cant, the rhetoric of causes, right or left, conservative or liberal, that bamboozles and deadens our ability to discriminate between likeness and difference so that freedom is slavery and war is peace, be it conducted by the bombing of Vietnam or the Old Rimrock post office. That the voice of Swede Levov so affirms the promise of America in the midst of a critique of its betrayal by Merry makes *American Pastoral* a central part of a canon whose dynamic of chastising the radical left as well as a repressive right can make this literature no more troubling than one of Lou's letters of protest ranting against LBJ and Nixon or a coffin borne at the end of the Fourth of July parade in Brookside.[7]

4. Fig Leaf: The Voice of the Pastoral

The voice of the star character in *American Pastoral*—the voice of Swede Levov—is not the voice of ripping off the fig leaf. His argot is not the argot of the streets of Newark where he was born and raised but the well-off suburb or more akin to the chatter we can imagine the "Ivan Ilyches" of Old Rimrock exchanging at the clubhouse after trooping back there from a round of golf. It is not the vernacular voice of a Huck Finn or the rap voice of a Tom Paine, Sam Adams or Frederick Douglass "sticking it to the man" or the irreverent voice of a Lenny Bruce or even the laconic, straight talk of a John Wayne as a cowboy and soldier in his films, all of which have been such animating voices of American politics and culture. It does not sound the dissonance of dissent of a coffin in a parade or a verbal bomb of protest as does the voice of his daughter, Merry. Instead, it is the voice of politeness that is the manner of the suburb. It is the voice that values the approval of authority and masters it to become president of a corporation and a country club. It is the friendly, handshaking, sometimes garrulous, voice of the fraternity. We can imagine Dawn Dwyer using a version of it to win Miss New Jersey. It has been the brick and mortar for creating the walled garden of so many restricted, exclusive places in America, some of which began tumbling down in 1960s America. It seems to have become second nature to Swede, but not to his brother Jerry, who, with their father, Lou Levov, are the animating, dissonant voices that become more vociferous at the end of the second section of *American Pastoral* entitled "The Fall."

Merry has her stutter; Jerry and Lou do not. They are the voices of disorder against the order Swede tries to construct in Old Rimrock. Swede meets his daughter in Newark where she is working in a forlorn part of the city that has become "dead" to Swede after the riots. She has become a convert to Jainism, wears a veil, and remains hidden from her father, who cannot understand why she detests him. When they meet, it is the ancient story of Orpheus, the builder of a walled city, against its destroyer— the savage, the barbarian, the violent, the Furies: "They are crying intensely, the dependable father whose center is the source of all order, who could not overlook or sanction the smallest sign of chaos—for whom keeping chaos far at bay had been intuition's chosen path to certainty, the rigorous daily given of life—and the daughter who is chaos itself" (p. 231). This is Herman Melville's Captain Vere siding with Orpheus against disorder, fearful of revolutionary protest. "With mankind," Captain Vere would say, "forms, measured forms, are everything; and that is the important couched in the story of Orpheus with his lyre spellbinding the wild denizens of the wood."[1] Brookside was created and protected by the "measured forms" of its zoning laws and the "decorum" of post office politeness that kept out the encroachment of Mt. Freedom and its Jewish denizens, and all of those who rioted inside Newark, and Merry and Jerry and Lou Levov know this.

"'Come in and strip it. Whatever's left, strip it, steal it, sell it,'" exclaims Lou to explain the fall of Newark.

> Stripping stuff—that's the food chain. Drive by a place where a sign says this house is for sale, and there's nothing there, there's nothing to sell. Everything stolen by gangs in cars, stolen by the men who roam a city with shopping carts, stolen by thieves working alone. The people are desperate, and they take anything. They "go junkin'" the way a shark goes fishing.
>
> "If there's one brick still on top of the other," cried his father [Lou], "the idea gets into their heads that the *mortar* might be useful, so they'll push them apart and take *that*. Why not? The mortar! Seymour, this city isn't a city—it's a carcass! Get out!" (p. 235)

Even the cobblestones from the streets are torn up. Seymour's visit to his daughter becomes the occasion for an ubi sunt lament about Newark, an elegy. But where he escapes to, Old Rimrock, has now also become a fallen world for him, with its order, security, even mortar, ripped apart by the bomb planting of his daughter, who he remembers, before the bomb, "blasting away at the dinner table about the immorality of their bourgeois life" (p. 240). Swede cannot take this ranting seriously, inclined as he is to defend "the moral efficacy of the profit motive," the same motive that he does not see now "tearing down" Newark in the aftermath of the riots just as it built it up during the time of his father creating the Newark Maid glove company and factory (p. 240). It is this profit motive that sent so many factories outside of Newark to the sun belt and then overseas, decimating the blue-collar jobs in a city that sustained a Black and white and immigrant working class. Swede sees his daughter—on whom he spent "tens of thousands of dollars' worth of orthodontia, psychiatry, and speech therapy—not to mention ballet lessons and riding lessons and tennis lessons"—tyrannized over "by the thinking of crackpots"—Communists, Weathermen, Jains—while Merry stutters out the same complaint against Swede: "*You're* the living example of the person who *never* thinks for himself! . . . You're the most conformist man I ever met! All you do is what's expec-expec-expected of you! . . . It's being a s-s-stupid aut-aut-aut-aut-aut-automaton! A r-r-r-r-robot!" (pp. 240, 241).

5. Walled Garden

When Philip Roth returned to Newark post-1967, he saw a city in ruins, a place transformed almost beyond recognition. If Swede Levov were to return to Old Rimrock in 2024, fifty-six years after his daughter, Merry, blew up the post office with a bomb, he would see a place very much the same, a place that has resisted the currents of American history: the pastoral giving way to the commercial and whiteness to diversity. The population of Mendham Township has increased from 3,500 in 1960 to 6,014 in 2022 with a relatively small increase in diversity over this six decades (from 1–2 percent to 14 percent) and a significant increase in protected "open space," now accounting for 3,000 of its 11,000 acres.[1] There is no commerce in the town center except a gift store called Harmony Brookside Gifts & Gallery attached to the post office that now sells coffee on the weekend.

A city is always something of a walled garden, even small towns such as Brookside, and its walls are the walls of zoning laws. Mendham Township's official website until 2021 described the motives of the town's planning efforts in a bucolic way: To preserve its "homes, farm buildings, and villages" in a "natural setting, away from the 'dark satanic mills' of the big city" keeping it "a portrait of Americana."[2] The only places zoned for business in Mendham Township are small spaces in the center of Brookside consisting of two buildings and a house in between them. The historical trajectory of Brookside reverses the trajectory of so many stories told about cities and towns in the United States including the narrative arc of Allen Ginsberg's poem, "Garden State." The endemic trajectory is the story of "paradise lost": a garden state fallen into the corruption that comes inevitably with development, expansion, sprawl. The trajectory of Brookside is the reverse: it has its origins as a small industrial town that became a garden suburb and now aspires to be a paradise regained, a place free from "satanic mills" and dedicated to "open space."[3] In the center of town on East Main Street, near the entrance to the Community Club, is an information sign erected by the Morris County Heritage Commission entitled "Brookside Historic District: Water Street" that reads: "Water power and natural resources made this a busy industrial village from the early 18th century through 1900. Visible today are the waterways that powered saw mills, grist mills, wagon shops, a glass factory and cottage industries."[4] The official website of Morris County, New Jersey in a section entitled "Historic Maps" lists under Mendham Township an 1868 map that updates the historical marker in the center of town by providing a business directory for Brookside in 1868 that includes a wagon manufacturer, blacksmith, miller, woolen manufacturer, and tannery. The map lists homes by owner and locations of businesses, and has an inset that also features the streams in the Mendhams that form some of the headwaters of the Passaic River. On the map, one river is named "Passaic River."[5]

In 1996, the Mendham Township Committee commissioned Acroterion, a consulting company on historical preservation, to prepare an application to the U.S. Department of the Interior to register Brookside on the National Register of Historic Places. The report provides an excellent short history of Brookside from its origins in the mid-eighteenth century to the 1920s.[6] It details—and illustrates with a set of maps—how Brookside began as a water-powered small-industry town whose residences first developed linearly alongside its brooks on East and West Main Street and up Woodland Road and down along Tingley Road, locating its original saw mills and grist mills and the tannery as well as its first buildings: the general store that became also the post office, the school in the building that was moved to become the Community Club, the municipal building, and the Union chapel that became its Congregational church. It specifies too how the town became the home of more industries into the late nineteenth century including a woolen mill, iron works, a glass factory, a shoe shop, and how for a few decades the Rockaway Railroad traveled alongside the banks of its main stream with a small station in the center of Brookside as it brought products of farms and orchards to urban markets. This railroad, nicknamed the Rock-a-Bye Baby, had two more stations in Mendham Township, one at Day's Hill near the end of Tingley Road and one at Pitney Farm near its border with Mendham. It also transported pupils in Brookside and from Ralston, Mendham, and Chester and even further west from the Pottersville area to Morristown High School. The fruit industry in the area, however, was damaged severely by the San Jose peach scale blight, which ruined the Rock-a-Bye Baby's best source of revenue (it transported 100,000 baskets of peaches in 1892), making this never-profitable railroad even less profitable. The rail line was purchased by Frank B. Allen in 1905 for $27,000; he was the last owner and salvaged it for scrap for $125,000 near the start of World War I, turning by far its best profit. Out past the fence for the baseball field in the center of town and along Harmony Brook, kids in the early 1960s could still hunt for and sometimes discover a rusted spike from this railroad, transporting them into an almost unimaginable era of an unpastoral Brookside.

Significantly, the Acroterion report adds how the town was transformed in the 1920s by commercial real estate development: "Brookside was taken over, quite literally, by a few businessmen in the 1920s who saw not only charm but real estate potential in this small rural village within driving range of northern New Jersey's metropolitan centers."[7] Brookside then became in the words of the report an "ex-urban enclave, informally restored to

Postcard of Brookside center featuring the post office, the municipal building, the Community Club, and the Congregational church. Photography and design by Judy Herndon. (Author's collection.)

Rock-a-Bye Baby Railroad station in the center of Brookside. The Mendham Township Committee, Brookside, New Jersey.

Rock-a-Bye Baby Railroad traveling through Washington Valley, Mendham Township. The Mendham Township Committee, Brookside, New Jersey.

radiate the image of an ideal early American village."[8] The descriptive history of the town in this report concludes: "The tree shaded roads and babbling brook offer pastoral beauty, giving no hint of the noisy, bustling village of the 19th century which used the brooks to power large mills."[9]

The story of the territory in Brookside called Dismal Harmony is as paradigmatic for the history of Mendham Township as it is un-paradigmatic for so much of the Garden State. The first owner of Dismal Harmony was Colonel John Evans, who purchased 1,666 acres, including all of Brookside, in 1716. One of the earliest developers of this property was Henry Clark, a Scotchman, who came to Brookside in 1727. In 1759 he built a dam and sawmill at the head of Dismal Glen, close to the border between Mendham Township and Mt. Freedom and in the present location of Woodland Lake. Along the other stream in the area—Harmony Brook—that traverses down through the Dismal Harmony area toward Main Street, Stephen Earl Connet built a sawmill in 1842, and he manufactured lumber and peach baskets. Dismal Brook was then tapped to power two sawmills, a woolen mill, and two gristmills as well as a forge. The Dismal Harmony area was also logged for lumber and charcoal. As steam power replaced waterpower, the industry in Brookside powered by Dismal and Harmony Brooks began to disappear. A small village called Harmony, below the headwaters of Harmony Brook, disappeared too as the village became the location for the Clyde Potts reservoir in the 1930s.[10] No *Chinatown* film will be scripted about the disappearance of Harmony, but control over the water is the story of the development of Brookside as much as it is the story of the development of Los Angeles. Mendham Township, however, does a double cross on the story of *Chinatown*. In Mendham Township, real estate deals do not open farmland to commercial development. Instead, these deals end small industry and fend off commerce for the transformation of the town into a picturesque village and its woodland and farmlands into suburban housing developments and estates. But even this real estate transformation faced its limits—or exclusions—in order to preserve open, green space.

In 1967, the Otto Badenhausen family, after the death in 1966 of Otto who had acquired the P. Ballantine and Sons Brewing company of Newark with his brother, Carl, in 1933, decided to sell 77 of the 300 acres it owned near the center of Brookside, including land near the top of Stoney Hill Road where the Reisner family lived surrounded by the woodlands and wetlands called Dismal Harmony. Dr. David J. Reisner and his wife, Muriel, joined with other residents of Stoney Hill Road, including my father and members of the planning board, to help lead the effort to protect this land as open space. The Reisners and other citizens in the neighborhood raised an initial deposit for the land, and then they were able to persuade the North Jersey Conservation Foundation to be an interim purchaser pending state and federal funding. Loans and gifts from other residents in Mendham Township made it possible for the conservation foundation to purchase the land. Then New Jersey's new Green Acres program purchased 50 percent of the land and the remaining 50 percent was purchased with federal Department of Housing and Urban Development funding. Since 1967, Dismal Harmony has been expanded to 146 acres, and Mrs. Badenhausen donated another 198 acres of her property adjacent to Dismal Harmony to the Morris County Park Commission. The protected natural area now comprises 344 acres. Trails into this area—and throughout the township— have been dubbed Patriot's Path, where people love to walk and bike in the woods.

Brookside from the 1950s into the 1970s had a vibrant community marked by its celebrated annual Fourth of July parade sponsored by the Community Club that included contests in fire ladder raising, skeet shooting, horseshoes, frog jumps, turtle races, pie eating, an egg toss, Little League baseball, and a father-son softball game.[11] Just as Newark had its public library and Ruppert Stadium that served the young book-loving and baseball-loving Philip Roth, Brookside had a public library inside its municipal building run mostly by volunteers and a men's baseball team in the Morris & Somerset league that would attract twenty-five to forty fans to its wood-plank stands for Sunday afternoon home games. The team's stars included

Coach Sam Tufts, Walter Earl (the catcher and my sixth-grade math teacher), Pete Hawkins, and Bob Major, the son of a former principal of Mendham Township Elementary School whose mother taught third grade at the school (and I played shortstop in some games). Up into the 1970s there was a working dairy farm on West Main Street close to the elementary school and for many years in the back of one home a little goat farm almost within smell of the municipal building.

The town center has changed very little, although its surrounding farmland and some of its wooded spaces have been developed further into garish huge homes trumpeting economic success. But the combination of exclusive zoning dating back to planning in the mid-1930s and insider power tapping into the first use of the state's new Green Acres funds has preserved its greenness and its overwhelming—85 percent of the demographic—whiteness. Of the town's 11,000-plus acres, 3,000 are now "open space" areas protected from development, and every other area has been "protected" so far by zoning restrictions from affordable housing in the form of apartment units. The median selling price for a house in Brookside's 07926 zip code, according to *Forbes Magazine* in 2009, was $3,121,115, making Brookside the tenth most expensive place for a home in the nation, although another source now lists the median selling price in this zip code at $680,900.[12]

Brookside is one of the three main neighborhoods—Ralston and Washington Valley are the other two—within Mendham Township, which surrounds Mendham Borough like a wrench head around a nut. The two parts were once together as one political entity, incorporated on March 29, 1749, by the Morris County Court. But

Mendham Township broke apart into two pieces in 1906 in a dispute among residents about funding a municipal improvement—a public water and sewage system—that one side (what became the Borough) favored and the other side that remained Mendham Township did not. This antipathy between the municipalities continued in different forms. Mendham Borough had a range of businesses in its town center—some dating back to the late eighteenth century including the Blackhorse Inn—and unlike Mendham Township, it continued to encourage business development, opening a shopping center in the mid-1960s. Mendham Borough felt it could lower taxes by having more businesses in the town, and it was open to rental apartments. People in Mendham Township, on the other hand, were mostly willing to pay higher taxes than those in Mendham Borough to keep business development out of the town.[13]

Nathan Zuckerman in Roth's *The Counterlife* argues that he "could not think of any historical society that had achieved the level of tolerance institutionalized in America or that had placed pluralism smack at the center of its publicly advertised dream of itself," and he celebrates America as a "country that did not have at its center the idea of exclusion" (C, p. 54). The history of Brookside also serves as a reminder about the degree to which Zuckerman's celebration of America in *The Counterlife* is belied so much by the history of Brookside and the social practices of its inhabitants who embraced an exclusiveness that was a combination of tacit social fiat and de jure zoning. This exclusiveness de jure began with the inception of zoning laws in the late 1930s to the early 1940s. Mendham Township disallowed multifamily homes and apartments and prohibited commercial properties: businesses and hotels. These laws had an unwritten hidden agenda. They were designed in part to prevent the spread into Mendham Township of the Jewish resort town that bordered Mendham Township called Mt. Freedom. As Bucky Robinson and Lou Levov in *American Pastoral* know and express, there were "haters" out there in the territory, and those haters knew how to build walls. This history of Brookside— beneath whatever fig leaf or myth or dream might hide it— is the story of America that is also the story of *American Pastoral*: At the heart of this town is the point-counterpoint story of an America committed at once to the dream fantasy of inclusion and the practice of exclusion.[14]

In 1960, Brookside was 99 percent white, an iconic Wonder bread and Ivory soap place. "By 1960," the historian Lisabeth Cohen writes, "New Jersey had distinguished itself as a highly suburbanized state, particularly within the New York metropolitan area."[15] Seventy percent of the state's total land area, Cohen notes, qualified as suburban, making New Jersey along with Connecticut the two most suburbanized states in the United States. Cohen adds that "Northern New Jersey, host to much of the state's suburban expansion, evolved into a complicated mosaic arranged in a pattern of solid white only occasionally punctuated by distinct, and intense, areas of black."[16] But within this whiteness, there were shades of difference as well as a pocket or two of brown as well as Black. Among the neighboring and nearby towns, Mendham Borough had its share of Italian Americans. Dover had a large Latino population, mostly Puerto Rican. Mt. Freedom was largely Jewish. Randolph was a mix of white ethnicity including Italian American and Jewish (mostly all working class). Chester was still in part a German American farm town. Morristown was significantly

Irish American and African American with its WASP upper class in the areas where Morristown extended to Harding Township and New Vernon. Nearly bordering Mendham Township are Bernardsville, Far Hills, and Bedminster. The territory of these three towns in the 1960s was East Egg compared with Brookside's West Egg. Here was old money. Brookside was more nouveau riche with some small pockets of working class. Folks in the town referred to the people in Bernardsville as "Bernardsville British." Far Hills is home to the headquarters for the U.S. equestrian team and is near the home of the United States Golf Association. Jackie Kennedy bought a home in Far Hills and participated in events of its Essex Hunt Club, which sponsored the Far Hills steeplechase horse race. It has areas zoned for a minimum of a ten-acre lot, double that until recently of the largest zoned lot in Mendham Township. Bedminster is home to the Trump National Golf Club, which became Donald Trump's extension to the White House during his presidency.[17]

Philip Roth in an interview with a French journalist in 1981 describes his neighborhood in the Newark of his coming of age as an ethnic enclave surrounded by other enclaves: "I lived in a predominantly Jewish neighborhood and attended public schools where about 90 percent of the pupils and teachers were Jewish. To live in an ethnic or cultural enclave like this wasn't unusual for an urban American child of my generation" (RMO, p. 106). He then notes the change: "Newark is now a predominantly black city in a nightmarish state of decay, but until the late fifties it was demographically divided up like any number of American industrial cities that had been heavily settled in the late nineteenth and early twentieth centuries by waves of immigration from Germany, Ireland, Italy, Eastern Europe, and

Russia." He adds, "As soon as they could climb out of the slums where most of them began in America, more or less penniless, the immigrants formed neighborhoods within the cities where they could have the comfort and security of the familiar while undergoing the arduous transformations of a new way of life. These neighborhoods became rivalrous, competing, somewhat xenophobic subcultures within the city; each came to have an Americanized style of its own" (RMO, pp. 106–107) Roth thus explains that coming of age he "grew up feeling a part of the majority composed of the competing minorities, no one of which impressed me as being in a more enviable social or cultural position than our own" (RMO, p. 107).

What is so resonant in Roth's description of Newark is that, however much it stands in stark contrast to the stereotype of western Morris County as a homogeneous white spot, the configuration of the towns that neighbored Brookside and that comprised the towns with baseball teams against which Brookside played in Little League and Babe Ruth competitions—e.g., Mendham Borough, Chester, Long Valley, Flanders, Far Hills, Randolph, Gladstone, Peapack, Mine Hill—represented in many ways, like the Newark that Roth remembers, neighborhoods that were "rivalrous, competing, somewhat xenophobic subcultures." Again, in Roth's words, there were towns, like Brookside and Far Hills and Bernardsville, with an exceptionalist self-regard, each of which provided to some degree "the comfort and security of the familiar," even if that "familiar" was more the familiarity of class as well as ethnicity. But differences of ethnicity and religion also figured in composing lines of demarcation and attitude. Unlike what Roth says about the neighborhoods of Newark, among the towns surrounding Mendham Township and among the neighborhoods composing Mendham Township itself—Brookside, Washington Valley, Ralston, and the so-called (by some) redneck district closest to Mt. Freedom—there were places that impressed its denizens "as being in a more enviable social or cultural position," and that place was the place where people had to pick up their mail from the post office: Brookside, 07926.

But nothing in America can zone out the berserk from any town or hamlet, however small, as Mary Austin, Sherwood Anderson, Sinclair Lewis, William Faulkner, and Flannery O'Connor, among others, have taught us. Merry Levov has a poster in her room that her father tore down three months after the bombing. The poster reads: "We are against everything that is good and decent in honky America. We will loot and burn and destroy. We are the incubation of your mother's nightmares." Its attribution: the "WEATHERMEN MOTTO" (p. 252). Merry concludes "that there could never be a revolution in America to uproot the forces of racism and reaction and greed" (p. 260). Swede, in his meeting with Merry in Newark, spews vomit on her. Their conversation ends, "If you love me, Daddy, you'll let me be" (p. 266). Swede tells his younger brother, Jerry, about his confrontation with Merry, including that Merry has killed three other people in Oregon. Jerry rips into Swede, condemning him for not taking Merry out of Newark, through physical force if necessary. There is a code of the street. Jerry gives us the "code" of Brookside, of the middle-class suburb that John Updike depicts in fiction as well as anybody. Jerry continues to lambaste Swede: "You keep yourself a secret. Nobody knows what you are. You certainly never let *her* know who you are. That's what she's been blasting away at—that façade. All your fucking *norms*. Take a good look at what she did to your *norms*" (p. 275). Jerry does not let up. "You win the trophy. You always make the right move. You're loved by everybody. You marry Miss New Jersey, for God's sake. There's thinking for you. Why did you marry her? For the appearance. Why do you do everything? For the appearance!" (p. 275).

This is the critique of the suburban world that becomes a 1960s cliché, just as it was a cliché in the 1920s in the critique of Main Street by Sinclair Lewis and just as it is a critique of the so-called progressive world of America, the city on a hill as façade, as appearance, as cover-up. Underneath lies what is revealed in a classic *New Yorker* cartoon by Donald Reilly: One pilgrim on a Mayflower-like ship with land in sight says to another, "Religious freedom is my immediate goal, but my long-range plan is to go into real estate."[18] Not a city on a hill, but a nice home—a very nice home—on Main Street, in an Arcadian world, is the end of the pilgrim's progress and Thomas Jefferson's vision of how America could sustain its garden state world, set off from the vice of the city, by remaining the home of the agrarian farmer, which Dawn becomes, raising cattle on her farm on Arcady Hill Road. But Merry bombs the heart of Old Rimrock just as the rioters in Newark destroy old Newark for the Levovs.

Part II

Babel

● ● ● ● ● ● ● ● ● ●

6. All Babel Breaks Loose

American Pastoral unmuffles America in the 1960s. The diatribe of Jerry against Seymour's "façade" world concludes the second section, "The Fall," and prefaces the last section, "Paradise Lost." At the end of "The Fall," the walls of the garden come tumbling down and the "snakes" are exposed. For Jerry Levov, the tumbling down begins with Seymour falling in love with "Miss New Jersey," Dawn Dwyer, the Mick from Elizabeth. For Lou, the father, the fall is the fall of Newark in the riot of 1967. For Seymour "Swede" Levov, the fall comes with the bombing of the post office by his daughter, Merry. He had left Newark for Old Rimrock in full transcendentalist mode, full of Emersonian wonder for the garden state of nature, seduced by a romance vision of a life in Old Rimrock that would transcend the fault lines scarred deep beneath the cobblestone streets of Newark: the divisions of race and religion and class that segregated the city in shards and bred the fears and resentments that Swede and so many other residents sought to flee after 1967. But Babel breaks loose in Old Rimrock too in 1968 with the sound and fury of Merry's dissonance inside the Levov home and then her bomb inside the post office.

The "Paradise Lost" section is set several years later, in 1973–1974, after the fall of Newark and amid the fall of President Richard Nixon. The Levovs have sold the cows, and they are planning to a build a new home. Bill Orcutt, a country squire whose family has a deep history in Morris County extending back to the colonial era, is its architect. Lou, the father, makes no change. He is up in arms again against another president, Nixon. In the 1960s, he was up in arms against Lyndon Johnson and engaged in an incessant letter-writing campaign against Johnson and the Vietnam War, just as the colonists in the 1770s engaged in an incessant campaign of petitions to King George III and Parliament. Lou is as unsuccessful in his protests as the colonists were. In the words of Jefferson's draft of the Declaration of Independence, England was "deaf to the voice of justice & of consanguinity," and he condemned them as "unfeeling brethren."[1] This deafness justified the action of the Declaration and the formal commencement of the Revolutionary War.

Merry is an apple that has not fallen far from the tree in Old Rimrock if that tree is rooted in the example of her grandfather. She too participates in a letter-writing campaign in protest against Lyndon Johnson and the Vietnam War. She and her grandfather are their own Committee of Correspondence. But this letter-writing campaign has no chance of success in Merry's eyes: "J-j-johnson's a war criminal. . . . He's not going to s-s-s-stop the w-w-war, Grandpa, because you tell him to" (p. 288). "He's also a man," Lou responds, "trying to do his job, you know" (p. 288). Merry counters in riposte: "He's an imperialist dog. . . . There's no d-d-d-difference between him and

Hitler" (p. 288). Lou disagrees with his daughter, arguing that she exaggerates and pointing out the differences between Johnson and Hitler. "I *gotta* be political with the guy, sweetheart. I can't write the guy and call him a murderer and expect that he's going to listen" (p. 289). The grandfather then goes into a history lesson for his granddaughter, "Believe me, I know what it is to read the newspaper and start to go nuts" (p. 289). He tells her about the pro-Nazi, pro-Hitler sympathies of Father Coughlin, Charles Lindbergh, Mr. Gerald L. K. Smith, and the politics of Joseph McCarthy, Westbrook Pegler, Raymond Cohn: the political figures that Roth writes against in his *Plot Against America* and *I Married a Communist*. For Lou, the grandfather, as for Milan Kundera and for Philip Roth, the struggle against power is the struggle of memory against forgetting, and through Lou and his letter-writing campaign—and his history lecture to his granddaughter—he is offering the disillusionment of history against any belief in a pastoral vision of America in the mid-twentieth century, the era before and after the Good War of World War II. Lou momentarily loses his grip and suggests to Merry that she "join the *other* side," giving as an example Benedict Arnold (p. 290). Lou and Merry continue to trade opinions about the anti-war opposition of Bobby Kennedy, Eugene McCarthy, Frank Church, and J. William Fulbright, whom Merry calls a "racist" (p. 290). Merry's memory appears to go deeper, back to the Revolutionary tradition in New Jersey. "Merry feels it's all gone beyond writing letters to the president" (p. 291). The apple does not fall far from the tree in the Garden State. Here may be the home of the Levovs on Arcady Hill Road. But here too is the home of General Washington and his army for two winters—the home of revolutionary violence—and Merry's strike against the post office seems to be another strike, similar to the "shot heard round the world" and the Declaration of Independence, against the futility of letter writing—or protesting with words and through words—against the Vietnam War.

The "Paradise Lost" section of *American Pastoral* could also be called "Babel." It opens with the debate between Merry and her grandfather over the Vietnam War. Her dad, Swede, adds his two cents. Swede and his father also argue about whether or not to leave Merry alone, as Lou sees Merry as a danger to herself: "'We've got to nip this in the bud,' he confided to his son, 'This won't do, not at all'" (p. 288). But Swede tells her grandfather to leave her alone and not argue with her. The centerpiece of the "Paradise Lost" section in *American Pastoral* is a dinner party hosted by the Levovs and attended by Bill Orcutt, the architect with whom Dawn is having an affair, and his wife Jennifer; Barry Umanoff, a law professor at Columbia University and former teammate of Swede's at Weequahic High School, and his wife, Marcia Umanoff, a literature professor with strong opinions; and Shelley Salzman, a doctor, and his wife, Sheila, the speech therapist who had worked with Merry and had hid her in the days right after the bombing and with whom Swede has a four-month affair. Swede's wife, Dawn, is in emotional breakdown over the bombing by their daughter. Roth assembles this congress of voices at the Levovs' dinner party, and they engage in a debate about Nixon, Watergate, *Deep Throat* (the film), permissiveness, and the Garden of Eden, with Lou weighing in on this subject too: "That when God above tells you not to do something, you damn well don't do it—that's what. Do it and you pay the piper. Do it and you will suffer from it for the rest of your days" (p. 360).

The apple has been bitten, and innocence has been lost, all around this table. Bill is fucking Dawn, Swede fucked Sheila, and Jerry would say Seymour was fucked the moment he decided to marry Dawn. Marcia, the English professor, upholds transgression as a way of knowing, with Bill Orcutt objecting to William Burroughs and the Marquis de Sade and Jean Genet—the great outlaws—and "The Let Everyman Do Whatever He Wishes School of Literature," and "The brilliant school of Civilization Is Oppression and Morality Is Worse" (p. 365). "The outlaws are everywhere. They're inside the gates," concludes chapter 8 (p. 366). The next chapter is more dinner party talk. Swede looks at Bill Orcutt and sees "civilized savagery" and Dawn looks at him and sees "Wasp blandness" (pp. 383, 384). Swede remembers Thanksgiving dinners with Dawn's family, before her father, Jim Dwyer, died, when Lou and Jim, the grandfathers, with their "great memories," would meet, not so much to discuss Judaism and Catholicism, but Newark and Elizabeth, the two of them "swapping stories about what life had been like when they were boys" (p. 400). This riff concludes with the thought: "A moratorium on all the grievances and resentments, and not only for the Dwyers and the Levovs but for everyone in America who is suspicious of everyone else. It is the American pastoral par excellence and it lasts twenty-four hours" (p. 402). The grandfathers—Jim and Lou—find beautiful common ground, reminiscing about their almost common ground, the neighboring neighborhoods of Elizabeth and Newark. Divisions and differences are set aside in this remembering that is two parts history and one part nostalgia. The dream vision of America has long taken several forms including all of us sitting down at the table of brotherhood and another of the transformation of "the jangling discords of our nation into a beautiful symphony of brotherhood"—Babel giving way to Pentecost.[2] The "Paradise Lost" section of *American Pastoral* leaves us with Babel in an Edenic setting.

7. Inside the Territory: Myth and History

No place is innocent of myth or symbolism in the American cultural geography, but some places bear more of the burden of such mythology than others. Brookside on the face of it does not bear the burden of history, but it does bear the burden of myth. Swede Levov is not alone in his sense of wonder and hope for Old Rimrock as an Edenic place, a garden world or—better yet—a Pentecostal place where the differences of Babel that marked the city could be overcome. Just as the American West offered in the vision of Frederick Jackson Turner a redemptive place free from the racial divisions that fractionalized the country in divisions between the North and South, so too it seems does western Morris County offer Swede an escape from the anger, intolerance, prejudice, corruption, congestion, injustice, and rioting that split apart Newark in the middle of the 1960s.

Merry Levov is something of a "mute inglorious Milton" (in words from Thomas Gray's "Elegy from a Country Churchyard").[1] She is a revolutionary, with a stutter. She has trouble putting her dissonance into sentences that flow. She generalizes and makes a very problematical analogy: Lyndon Baines Johnson is Hitler. Merry's rebellious rhetoric smacks of the platitude of propaganda, the generalizations, the lack of particulars, the lack of what Roth embraces so dearly: a live, vibrant, original, complex, nuanced language grounded in a "passion for specificity."[2] There is an official language of government and there is an official language of protest. Toni Morrison is among the best of contemporary American writers, along with Roth, for expressing dissonance against such official language. Just like Roth in *Our Gang*, Morrison in her Nobel Prize acceptance speech cries out in protest against this official language, hurling her own arsenal of verbal bombs against it.[3] It is also the voice of Ralph Waldo Emerson protesting against "rotten diction" in *Nature* (1836) and George Orwell against Newspeak's "defense of the indefensible" in "Politics and the English Language" (1946) and Kenneth Burke against the rhetoric of Hitler's battle in *A Rhetoric of Motives*.[4] Merry is sixteen, too young in the eyes of Nathan Zuckerman to complicate, too young to compromise, and she is probably too young to plant a bomb, especially growing up in Old Rimrock, with no circle of co-conspirators, and with only the fury of her grandfather as an example, or the example of Paine and Washington.

Not knowing our history—or not minding much about each other's history, religion, ethnicity—appears to make it so much easier for people to mix and merge. This distancing of ourselves from our past, our roots, and the promise of liberation it affords is the promise of Old Rimrock to Swede, just as it was the promise of America to Jean-Jacques Crèvecoeur when he lyricized about America as a place where people could uproot themselves from the old world and make themselves anew, transplanted and revivified (thanks to the existence of land for the taking). The myth of the frontier for so long promised this too, and for Swede, Old Rimrock is a regenerative frontier, a place for re-genesis, and he is a "frontiersman" (p. 310). But, on the other hand, not knowing our history, or not caring to know what has been overcome—or who "we the people" dispossessed—or the history of people mixing and merging and intermarrying beyond old tribal affiliations, can also make it too easy to forget what has been learned, by trial and error and tragedy, in the process of America becoming America, the America that never was but that has been dreamed by Langston Hughes and Martin Luther King Jr. and many others before and after: an America that overcomes all that caused the racial divisions and inequalities that blew up Newark in 1967 and an America that foregoes the fakeness and the faux harmonies and the hypocrisies and the war crimes and cover-ups that helped lead Merry to plant a bomb in the Old Rimrock post office. What Merry's act reminds us of is that the old frontier of the West, as Richard Slotkin has revealed to us in his anti-pastoral American trilogy on the myth of the frontier, as well as the New Frontier of John F. Kennedy and Lyndon Baines Johnson, are places of "regeneration through violence" as was the Puritan errand into the wilderness and the Revolutionary War and the Civil War.[5] But the bombing of the post office by a young woman at the age of sixteen seems to be not just a protest against the politics and cover-ups that helped justify the Vietnam War. The comments by Lou and Jerry Levov as well as the dissonance that bubbled up among some students of the generation who came of age in Mendham Township in the 1960s suggest that Merry's bombing was also a protest against the cover-ups of the Levov family and their refusal to see the pretense of the pastoral in Old Rimrock, which Merry must have sensed somehow on the playgrounds of her school in Old Rimrock or in the halls of Morristown High School, just as Steven Cramer felt and remembered them in poems such as "The Parade, 1968" and in another poem of his entitled "For the Bullies of West Morris High."[6]

Roth describes the transformations of the 1960s as a critical moment of demythologization for America. He sees World War II, in which he came of age, as one of the great moments of mythologizing for America, and the 1960s as its counterpoint. This push and pull, this dialectic of mythologizing and demythologizing in American culture, is not an inevitable dialectic, as the catalysts to the mythologizing and demythologizing often turn around moments of war. Because America has been at war so many times since its foundation—beginning with wars of dispossession against the American Indian and then the birth of the United States from Revolutionary War and its "rebirth" or reconstruction in the Civil War—America has had mythologizing as a dominant trait. But it also has had a recessive trait of demythologizing that surfaced most prominently in the midst and wake of the first major war it lost: the Vietnam War. Cities—and even small towns, even very small towns such as Brookside—are also subject to mythologizing: the province, in Brookside, of its real estate brokers and environmental protectors and township committees. It also has its demythologizers, however subdued or quiet or stuttering. The demythologizing force in Brookside was, on the one hand, gossip, the sharing of secrets through the grapevine, and, on the other hand, the implosions and explosions of its children in their teens, such as the planting of the bomb by Merry Levov, as well now as the poetry of a Steven Cramer. *Goodbye to the Orchard* is the title of his second book of poetry.

But what is most unseen about Brookside or unheard directly is its environmental racism: the way that Mendham Township has used zoning ordinances and concerns

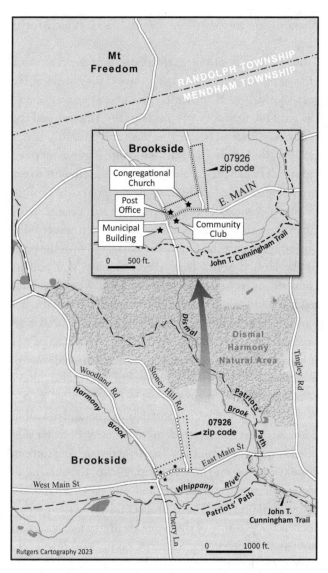

Map of Brookside center with inset featuring its brooks, buildings, and Dismal Harmony. Rutgers Cartography 2023, map by Michael Siegel.

Dismal Harmony falls. (Photo by Gregory M. Gustafson.)

over wetlands and the environment to protect not nature but its de facto exclusions implemented by its de jure legislation aided and abetted by its power and resources to get county money and state money and New Jersey Conservation Foundation funds to create park and recreation spaces or hundreds upon hundreds of acres of green space and fifty-five miles of trails through this space now called

Patriot's Path. Patriotic pride is much easier to feel walking the trails of Patriot's Path than walking by Weequahic High in Newark today. It is easier to feel patriotism when you are on the winning side of a war, when government serves your interests, and perhaps even more than Merry Levov could know and feel about Old Rimrock, Brookside is a place where government served the interests of the powerful and the privileged, and their interest was to preserve Brookside as it is.

8. Harmony: Bill Orcutt's WASP History Tour

In the "Paradise Lost" section, Roth introduces us more to Bill Orcutt and to Bucky Robinson, an optician who had played quarterback for Hillside High, the rival of Weequahic, and with whom Swede meets up at a touch football game Bill Orcutt hosts in his backyard on weekends. Each of them gives Swede a ride through the history of Morris County from their respective viewpoints. Orcutt gives the first tour. He is president of the local landmarks society and a conservationist with a bumper sticker that reads, "Morris Green, Quiet, and Clean" (p. 301). His family is from a prominent legal family in Morris County, with a long line of lawyers, judges, and state senators in the family. Orcutt had been a leader in the opposition that began in 1959 and lasted into the mid-1960s to the creation of a new airport in the part of New Jersey called the Great Swamp, not far from Brookside in the region that has New Providence as its center. For part of a social studies lesson at Mendham Township Elementary School, when I was in fourth grade, we all had to write letters to somebody—probably a state official—expressing our opposition to plans to build a jetport in this Great Swamp region. Many Brooksiders were part of this opposition just as some would later be fierce opponents of building a new a jail for Morris County on the border of Morris Township and Mendham Township. The opposition to the jetport led Congress to enact legislation to create the Great Swamp National Wildlife Refuge and this region would continue to be the site where power and influence in the 1960s tapped into a developing environmental conscience to protect places in the Garden State that were least subject to the toxic dangers of its industries and the fall of its old industries. Orcutt takes Swede on a history tour of Morris County that begins in the northwest corner of the county and then backtracks following "the southward meandering spine of the old iron mines" when "iron was king" (p. 302). Here is the town where Ironia Road, which courses through Mendham Township, leads to Mine Hill. Orcutt also shows Swede the old mills in Boonton where "axles, wheels, and rails were manufactured for the original Morris and Essex Railroad" (p. 302). Boonton in the 1960s appeared to be a busted down place with no business but a 7-Eleven and a liquor store surrounded by crumbling old brick factory buildings. It was an early example of what was happening to Paterson and Camden and Newark on a larger scale: deindustrialization.

Brookside too, long before Boonton, had its own moment of deindustrialization. For over three decades from the 1880s to circa 1917, it had a railroad running through it: the Rock-a-Bye Baby Railroad. Orcutt explains this as well to Swede, noting how a railroad had run from Whitehouse Station through Brookside and on into Morristown as part of a peach boom. Orcutt shows Swede Washington's Headquarters and then his tour wends its way back into an understanding for Swede of the source and trajectory of the Morris Canal, which makes a connection between the hometowns of Orcutt and Swede. The canal in its course through Newark traversed within a hundred yards of the Newark Maid factory before emptying into the Newark Bay. Completed to Newark in 1831, the canal thrived as a carrier of anthracite coal from Pennsylvania's Lehigh Valley to the iron industries of northern New Jersey and its industrializing eastern cities, but then fell into decline with the rise of railroad transportation, oil and trucking, its operation ending in 1924. A Morris Canal Greenway is now in development, yet it is Roth in *American Pastoral* who in part uses the canal as a reminder, in the narrative's words, of "the grander history of the state" (p. 303) and of a pre-pastoral era for western Morris County when it had in the words of John T. Cunningham an "iron backbone."[1]

Orcutt's tour also gives Swede a perspective on the source and trajectory of the inherited privilege of this country squire with its roots deep in the eighteenth century. Orcutt takes him out to a church cemetery dating back to the American Revolution where soldiers killed during the war were buried. This is the cemetery of the Hilltop Presbyterian Church in Mendham Borough, where, as Orcutt notes, rain from one side of the roof runs into the Passaic River and rain from the other runs into the Raritan. Here are primary headwaters of both rivers. Orcutt adds his own personal history to this tour of the cemetery, pointing out the grave of the first Morris County Orcutt, who arrived from northern Ireland in 1774 and fought at the Second Battle of Trenton. He brings the extensive history of his family in Morris County up to date with mention of how his grandfather buried in this cemetery had been classmates with Woodrow Wilson at Princeton. Swede's knowledge of his ancestry, on the other hand, goes back no further than his grandparents.

The first primary counterpoint to Orcutt's tour and history is provided by Lou Levov, as the novel gives us his reaction to the home in Old Rimrock that Swede bought. Lou wants Swede and Dawn to settle into the Newstead development in South Orange, New Jersey, buying a home in a largely Jewish neighborhood rather than out in a part of New Jersey that Lou describes as "a narrow, bigoted area" that is "rock-ribbed Republican" and where the Ku Klux Klan burned crosses on the property of people (p. 309). Lou adds, "And this is where the haters live, out here" (p. 309). But Swede, "like some frontiersman of old," would not be turned back from settling in the occupied territory of WASP privilege near where Jackie Kennedy would ride horses and go on fox hunts (p. 310). The frontier, Patricia Limerick reminds us, is not where we all escaped each other. It is where we all ran into each other.[2] It is a contact zone, a place often of violent conflict, a place where dominant power is replicated, not overcome or escaped. Swede is as innocent as Huck when he first lights out from the Widow Douglas: "I'm sure we'll find plenty of people out here who won't assert the superiority of the Protestant way the way their fathers and mothers did. Nobody dominates anybody anymore," Swede says (p. 311). He adds, "That's what the war was about. Our parents are not attuned to the possibilities, to the realities of the postwar world, where people can live in harmony, all sorts of people side by side no matter what their origins. This is a new generation and there is no need for that resentment stuff from anybody, them *or* us. And the upper class is nothing to be frightened of either. You know what you're going to find once you know them? That they are just other people who want to get along. Let's be intelligent about all this" (p. 311).

Swede's dream is the dream of so many in the most hopeful time of the early and mid-1960s. Merry's fury is fire and ice to this dream. Orcutt's own actions refute it too. His unsportsmanlike conduct against Swede in the touch football game—an act of cheating that serves as something of a preface to his affair with Dawn—provokes Swede who feels too that Orcutt has "looked down" on Dawn to dump him on his ass as he is scoring a touchdown against Orcutt's side, chortling to himself afterward, "Two hundred years of Morris County history, flat on its ass" (p. 381). But it is his teammate in this game, Bucky Robinson, who gives Swede's dream the most punishing reality check when he takes Swede on a Jewish history tour of the Old Rimrock region.

9. Dissonance: Bucky Robinson's Jewish History Tour

After Swede meets Bucky Robinson at a touch football game hosted by Orcutt, Bucky hitches a ride to a garage one day with Swede where his car was being repaired. Swede learns on the ride that Bucky is Jewish and had recently become a member of a temple in Morristown. Bucky, during the ride, gives Swede a history lesson that is the counterpoint to what Orcutt gives him. He informs Swede that Morristown had an "established Jewish community" that "went back to before the Civil War" and that "included quite a few of the town's influential people," among them the owner of the town's best department store and a trustee at Morristown Memorial Hospital who opened the door up to Jewish doctors (p. 313). Bucky also explains that as a child he "had been taken by his family up to Mt. Freedom, the resort town in the nearby hills, where they would stay for a week each summer at Lieberman's Hotel and where Bucky first fell in love with the beauty and serenity of the Morris countryside" (p. 313). "Up at Mt. Freedom," Bucky continues, "it was great for Jews: ten, eleven large hotels that were all Jewish, a summer turnover in the tens of thousands that was entirely Jewish—the vacationers themselves jokingly referred to the place as 'Mt. Friedman.'" Bucky adds, "If you lived in an apartment in Newark or Passaic or Jersey City, a week in Mt. Freedom was heaven" (p. 313). By the mid-1960s, this side of Mt. Freedom was mostly abandoned hotels, just a few still having guests, and one could see from the road the ruins of tennis courts overgrown with weeds and large pools, unfilled and cracked. It was impossible to imagine this place as a heaven, but Bucky reminds us it was. He then rips the fig leaf off: "But did the Swede know that before the war there'd been a swastika scrawled on the golf-course sign at the edge of Mt. Freedom? Did he know that the Klan held meetings in Boonton and Dover, rural people, working-class people, members of the Klan? Did he know that crosses were burned on people's lawns not five miles from the Morristown green?" (p. 314).[1]

Under the fig leaves of the garden world of Old Rimrock that Bucky Robinson rips off for Swede during his tour are more signs of antisemitism than Bucky himself knew in places juxtaposed alongside the environs of Dismal Harmony, an initial place first protected by New Jersey's Green Acres funds. Christopher Merrill has offered a beautiful description of the Tigris and Euphrates, the

Arcadia, the dark, sublime forest world of Dismal Harmony. Here is a brief passage:

> What was once a pleasant mix of farmers, blue collar
> workers, and business commuters to Manhattan has
> become a sanctuary for the rich and the famous. But what
> I remember now is the decision made by the community to
> establish a natural refuge called Dismal Harmony—almost
> 100 acres of woodland named after the pair of streams
> coursing through the property, Dismal Brook and
> Harmony Brook. It was the first parcel of land set aside in
> the state's Green Acres program, a prototype of the Nature
> Conservancy's efforts to preserve special places, and the
> village has since set aside 3,500 more acres.[2]

I discovered something else about Dismal Harmony and Brookside after I first read a report from 1936 of a committee chaired by William Alderson that would consider and then propose the first zoning ordinances for Mendham Township. Reading between its lines (and supplemented by oral history from my parents), the zoning laws originated in part as an effort to fence out the spread of Mt. Freedom into Mendham Township.

In 1937, down Woodland Road less than a mile from the center of town and the post office is a small dead-end road, Woodlawn Terrace, that entered the woods of Dismal Harmony on its west side. In the 1960s, this place was a small assortment of log cabins that once belonged to the Boy Scouts of America. In 1937 the main cabin was named Camp Swastika. Robert Baden Powell, the founder of the Boy Scouts, was influenced by Ernest Thompson Seton, founder of the Woodcraft Indians, which along with the Sons of Daniel Boone are the models that influenced

Powell, who published *Scouting for Boys* in 1908, which became one of the best-selling books of the twentieth century. Some very early scouting "Thanks" badges used the swastika as a symbol, and Baden Powell's biographer Michael Rosenthal argues that Powell used the swastika because he was a Nazi sympathizer, which others deny.[3] Whatever the reasons for Powell's use of the swastika, it is difficult to read the naming of Camp Swastika in an entirely innocent way or completely separate from the growth and development of Mt. Freedom, which one approached from the Brookside post office by traveling up Woodland Road, past Camp Swastika, which was located less than a mile from the bungalow communities of Mt. Freedom that were in Mendham Township land (on Shores Road and Levitan Lane off of Mt. Pleasant Avenue). Mt. Freedom could also be reached on foot by hiking up along Dismal Brook.

Not far from Mt. Freedom—fifteen miles away—in Andover Township, New Jersey was Camp Nordland, a center for the German American Bund from 1937 to 1941 when German Americans were, with Italian Americans, two of the largest ethnic groups in New Jersey. Camp Nordland was a 204-acre resort camp that opened on July 18, 1937 (and continued into 1941). The Bund held events at the facility to encourage pro-German, pro-Nazi values, with some of these events attracting over 10,000 visitors, and on August 18, 1940, it was the site of a joint rally of the Bund and the Ku Klux Klan.[4] *American Pastoral* takes us into the environs of the haters, but Bucky Robinson's tour of Mt. Freedom and the racial politics of zoning and environmentalism in Mendham Township—and Brookside as a diaspora from Newark—needs a few more stops.

Mt. Freedom in its heyday would have 10,000 visitors, with eleven hotels and forty-five bungalow colonies, summer camps, and swim clubs.[5] The resorts were all built within walking distance of the synagogue. The industry began in 1905 following the arrival of the Saltz, Levine, and Elgarten families. They each bought farmland but found they could not make a living from it and soon opened the first summer boarding houses for Jewish visitors from New York, many of whom were sent to Randolph by their doctors for clean air and healthful water. Bernard Hirschhorn, a wealthy New York garment maker, visited in 1917 and two years later bought one hundred acres of land and built the area's first bungalow colony. The rise and fall of Mt. Freedom as a primarily Jewish resort area is described by Karen Kominsky in a short essay in the *New Jersey Hills* newspaper. She reports, "Hotels which once featured the likes of Frank Sinatra, Henny Youngman, Buddy Rich, Phil Silvers, Red Buttons, George Jessel, Morey Amsterdam, Molly Picon, Baby Rose Marie, Joel Grey, Leslie Uggams, and other notables as their evening entertainment, found it more and more difficult to attract customers, who were beginning to journey further away, to the Catskills, to the Jersey Shore."[6] The hotels with their swimming pools and tennis courts were in ruins by the mid- to late 1960s, one of them becoming for a time the General Douglas MacArthur Military Academy. Some bungalow courts remained on the edge and inside the boundary of Mendham Township in the Shores Road and Levitan Lane areas—places with the lowest minimal lot size for a home in the township—nearby a lake whose overflow coursed into Dismal Brook and through the grounds of what was once probably the largest private estate in Mendham Township: the home of an industry magnate from Newark.

Otto Badenhausen, who owned the 330 acres that included the wooded areas in Dismal Harmony, made his fortune as a co-owner, with his brother, Carl, of the Ballantine Brewery in Newark, which they bought in 1933. It would become the third largest brewery in the United States in the post–World War II era. Their estate was at the dead end of Tingley Road, and the house in its size and location comes closest to the type of home where Swede Levov relocates his family from Newark. The Badenhausen family first moved to Brookside before World War II as part of the diaspora from Newark for the greener places of suburbia, a more pastoral place away from the factories and immigrant communities of the city. This is the diaspora of Swede Levov (as well as Chris Christie and Tony Soprano).

We can include in this diaspora from Newark Rabbi Joachim Prinz, whose remarkable life protesting antisemitism and for civil rights concluded with him living in Brookside. Born in Germany, Prinz served as rabbi for the Jewish community in Berlin beginning in 1925, where he was among the most outspoken from the beginning against the rise of the National Socialist party. He preached against the Hitler regime once it came to power and urged Jews to leave Germany for Palestine, which led to his expulsion from Germany in 1937. At the invitation of Rabbi Stephen Wise, he came to the United States, and in 1939 he was named rabbi of Temple B'nai Abraham in Newark, the second oldest Jewish congregation in New Jersey. This congregation itself moved from Newark to Livingston, New Jersey in 1973, and he continued to serve as

its rabbi until his retirement in 1977. Outspoken in the
United States as well as in Germany, Prinz fought against
racism and bigotry in America, and Roth makes him a
leading figure in Newark in his *Plot Against America*,
organizing protests against antisemitism and trying to protect Jews from the threat of pogroms during the reign of
President Lindbergh. Prinz was also a founding chairman
of the 1963 March on Washington, and he was the speaker
at the March who immediately preceded Reverend Martin Luther King Jr. and introduced him. From 1958 to
1966, Prinz served as president of the American Jewish
Congress. A biographical entry on Prinz concludes:
"Together with Hilde, he spent the final years of life in
their little cottage in Brookside, New Jersey—in a sense
returning to where he began, a small country village.
Joachim Prinz died September 30, 1988."[7] His home, at 20
Woodland Road, was one mile from the post office, two
miles from Mt. Freedom, and no more than several hundred yards from the former Boy Scout camp on the edge
of Dismal Harmony.

Ironically, some or most of the children of the families
whose parents came to Brookside for the serenity and
beauty of the place and to distance themselves from the
city, as does Swede Levov in *American Pastoral*, end up
reversing this diaspora. The price of homes and no apartment building rentals in Mendham Township make it very
difficult or impossible to afford. Old Rimrock strikes
Swede Levov as a paradise, but it was one with gates of
exclusion and prejudice that were invisible to him at first.
Inside there was the self-righteous contentment of those
who, in the words of Dana Johnson, were born on third
base and thought they had hit a triple or who had splashed
down in their backyard pool at the tail end of the pattern

that Nathan Zuckerman calls the "flight of the immigrant rocket": the "upward, unbroken immigrant trajectory from slave-driven great-grandfather to self-driven grandfather to self-confident, accomplished, independent father to the highest flier of them all, the fourth-generation child for whom America was to be heaven itself" (p. 122).[8] Jerry Levov mocks the flight of his brother and his wife to Old Rimrock as "their outward trip" into the United States where she could be "post-Catholic" and he could be "post-Jewish" and together they could raise "little post-toasties" (p. 73). For Merry, it appears, there was an all-too-harmonious side in the satisfaction that some people took in escaping into their castle worlds, moated off from the world of commerce and industry and from dissent against a war in Vietnam that was, as Frances Fitzgerald taught us in *Fire in the Lake*, destroying villages and the pastoral worlds in Southeast Asia in the name of saving them, bringing the machinery of war—including the bomb— into the garden, as Merry Levov would do in her own way in Old Rimrock and as sons and daughters of parents in Brookside did in carrying a coffin down Main Street and past the judging stand in front of the post office at the Brookside Fourth of July parade in 1969.[9]

10. Counterfactual: Beatrice and George Jenkins Sr.'s Black History Tour of Morristown

Swede Levov befriends Bucky Robinson playing touch football with Bill Orcutt, but he never befriends an African American in Old Rimrock, and no African American gives him a Black history tour of western Morris County. This is not a lapse on the part of Swede (however much its absence is revealing). In the 1960s there were no African Americans (to my knowledge) living in Brookside for a Swede to befriend. (The only African Americans I remember seeing in Brookside in this decade were employees of Waxin Jackson Floor Waxing company when they waxed the wooden floors of the Brookside post office and Mrs. Byrd, who worked as my family's cleaning lady once a week from the mid-1960s through the mid-1970s. She was from South Carolina and lived on Ridgedale Avenue in Morristown in one of the two main parts of its Black neighborhood and one that was almost within shouting distance of Washington's Headquarters and not far from Millionaire's Row along Morris Avenue.)

Merry Levov, however, as a student would have had daily contact during the school week with African Americans at Morristown High School, who composed 16–20 percent of the student body in those years. Roth takes some poetic license to make Merry a student at this high school. Technically, Merry, as a resident of Old Rimrock, would have attended high school at West Morris Regional High School in Washington Township, eighteen miles from Morristown and thirteen miles from Brookside. This high school opened in 1958. Before, high school students in Brookside attended Morristown High. The increasing number of African Americans at this school in the 1950s may have led in part to the decision to establish West Morris Regional High School. The increasing number of African American students did lead to a movement in the 1960s for Morris Township to make plans for a breakaway high school from Morristown for the students who lived in the wealthy, upscale, and very white neighborhoods of Morris Township called Harding and New Vernon. But an African American woman, Beatrice

Jenkins, president of the Morris County Urban League, joined as lead plaintiff with seven other Morristown residents in a legal case to prevent this separation. The decision in her favor made by the New Jersey Supreme Court in 1970 is regarded as a landmark school integration ruling not only in New Jersey but also the nation.[1] Legal historians have even called this a more successful decision than *Brown v. Board of Education* because it worked better in practice.[2] It kept Morristown High School an integrated school in numbers beyond symbolism, or it did so for a time.

In 1974, Morristown High School suffered the blowup of a racial incident with fights breaking out between Black and white students that required the intervention of seventy police officers to quell it. Then, probably not coincidentally, in May 1974, the Harding Township School District was given permission by the state commissioner of education to begin sending its students to Madison High School rather than Morristown starting with the 1975–1976 school year. Madison—the home of two universities, Fairleigh Dickinson and Drew—had a significantly smaller African American population. Madison itself suffered a notorious racial incident in 1964 when a white barber refused to cut the hair of African Americans. Some students at Drew University, both African American and white, joined the protest against this discrimination. The case went to the New Jersey Supreme Court, which decided against the owner of the barber shop.[3]

Beatrice's husband, George, rose to leadership positions within the Morristown police force, retiring as detective lieutenant after thirty years on the force. George and Beatrice both were leaders of the African American community of Morristown. George was an active member of the

Fair Housing Council, the Urban League, the NAACP, the American Cancer Society, and the American Red Cross, and was a business owner (A & B Cleaning Services), and he served for a time as the community service representative for Morristown High School. Notably, their oldest of three children, George Jenkins Jr., in words from the obituary for his father, "identified with the Black Panthers, and got arrested for peacefully protesting the Vietnam War in a town parade."[4] He has been a successful real estate professional in the Morristown area since 1978. His age would have made him a classmate of Merry at Morristown High School (a few grades above her). My own choice to lead Swede Levov on a Black history tour of western Morris County would be George and Beatrice Jenkins and their oldest son. The Vietnam War protests by George Jr. joins with the 1969 protest of the Fourth of July parade in Brookside and the protest by Vietnam Veterans Against the War in 1970 that originated in Morristown as nonfictional acts that are part of a rebellious tradition— if not of an "indigenous American berserk"—that have been undertaken in the footsteps of Washington and in the shadow of the figure of Thomas Paine in Morristown's Burnham Park fighting with words as his bullets and bombs.[5]

11. On the Dead-End Dirt Road: The Quiet Babel of Stoney Hill Road and Where Goodbye Newark Meets Goodbye Orchard

Swede Levov has a fantasy of himself living out in Old Rimrock as a new Johnny Appleseed. He walks sometimes five miles back and forth from his home on Arcady Hill

Road to the center of town, the post office. When he picks up the *Newark News* at the post office, he thinks this place has not changed since it began as a general store run by the Hamlins after World War I. Swede notes all the signs on the general store. He sees the store to be what it is pictured in the photo used on the front cover of the novel: "Kids sat on the steps of the store. Your girl would meet you there. A meeting place, a greeting place. The Swede loved it" (p. 317). Philip Roth presents Old Arcady Road in Old Rimrock for Swede Levov as his garden world that then has its fall. The only neighbors of the Levovs or other homeowners on Old Arcady Road we learn about in *American Pastoral* are the Orcutts. The Arcady Hill Road that Roth creates in Old Rimrock gives the feel of Old Rimrock as the home of a gentry class nowhere stratified. But Brookside in the 1960s still had as its oldest base a stratum of blue-collar families and longtime residents of Brookside going back generations that included its farmers and tradespeople, a citizenry juxtaposed against a nouveau riche that was often part of a diaspora from cities such as Newark and the boroughs of New York. My brief portrait that follows of families living on a road in the center of Brookside—Stoney Hill Road—offers a sense of what could be called the "quiet babel" inside this model of the pastoral place for Roth.[1]

I was born and raised near the center of Brookside on Stoney Hill Road, a dead-end dirt road whose almost disguised entrance at the foot of a steep rise off East Main Street was close to the Congregational church and across from the baseball field in the center of the town and very near a back entrance across two fields into Dismal Harmony. At its base, on the other side of East Main Street, were the stone ruins of an old building from the earlier small industry Brookside where we would search and dig for artifacts, sometimes finding shards of old glass bottles and old cans. In the 1960s, the road had fifteen homes inhabited mostly by families who were on the high side of the middle class and by two that were blue collar or working class. The professions included three bankers, two doctors, an ophthalmologist, three salesmen, a cement factory owner, an airplane pilot, a construction worker, a carpenter, and an elderly woman living on her own. At the bottom of the road, on the corner of Stoney Hill Road and East Main Street, facing the baseball field, was the home of a much-admired family doctor, an immigrant from Ukraine whose doctor's office was on the ground floor of the home and who lived there with his wife, a painter, and four children (and with carrier pigeons—a hobby of his— in his backyard). Across from our home was the ophthal-mologist with his office in Morristown and a wife who had a remarkable indoor garden of African violets in their cel-lar. They had two daughters who both attended Morris-town High School. One married a man who became a test pilot during the Vietnam War. They had two grandsons, one who died of meningitis, devastating the family. Up the hill, two houses away, lived a family with two teenagers who belonged to a very strict fundamentalist religion. The oldest daughter attended West Morris High School with my older sister and would sometimes come to our home in tears, distraught at the strictness of her parents who would not allow her to attend a school dance. Farther up the hill was the home of an airline pilot who landed a plane at Newark Airport when the wheels would not open for the landing. They sprayed the runway with foam. He kept the plane in the air until it was empty of fuel, and then he landed, without wheels, and no one was injured. A story about the incident appeared in *Reader's Digest*. At the end of a long driveway near us on the lower half of the road lived a tall, thin elderly man who resembled Abraham Lincoln and owned a specialty woodworking company in Morristown and kept beehives for honey adjacent to our backyard. He married a woman from the South whom he met through something of a lonely hearts club correspondence connection. His sister owned a home off the same driveway that became a rental property where the poet Christopher Merrill lived when young with his family (and as my next-door neighbor) for a time in the late 1960s or early 1970s.[2] The cement factory owner had a stylish modern house of glass walls facing the woods and a second home at the New Jersey shore in Mantoloking and a yacht. The doctor who lived at the very end of the road, with a home in the woods bordering Dismal Harmony, became a leading activist with his wife in lobbying the New Jersey government to protect Dismal Harmony from developers. The odd man out was the construction worker whose small home overlooked a former apple orchard he owned and refused to sell for subdivision. After his death, the orchard was sold off and became part of a subdivision with homes out of scale in opulence with any others on the road, a subdivision that included a field we called the Post's lot where my father would pasture his horse. There are inevitably as many stories on Stoney Hill Road as there are people who lived in these homes, and I will spare chronicling the stories of the affairs, the alcoholics, and the divorces on this road. Suffice it to say, Stoney Hill Road in the 1960s in a word had its own babel of stories as did every street in Brookside and Mendham and Morristown and Newark—and probably even Arcady Hill Road in Old Rimrock.

The center of Brookside still appears to have changed barely at all since the 1960s. The out-of-use gas pump is no longer in front of the post office. There is a second baseball field—specifically for Little League—next to the main baseball field. The township has added more buildings for fire trucks and ambulances in the back parts of the parking lot for the municipal building and a small home next door was bought and converted into the police station. In the 1960s, Mendham Township had two policemen, and now it has fifteen, with a ratio of police to population higher than Los Angeles despite a much lower crime rate that includes only one murder in the past seventy-five years: a grisly homicide arising, I was told, from a drunken fight among friends in a card game that produced a severed head—whose photograph I was shown by Donald O'Keefe, the chief of police, when the township clerk's office was testing the photocopying capabilities of a new copy machine. (Somehow, the meticulous researcher Roth learned about this murder and mentions it in *American Pastoral* in the one place in the novel where the name "Brookside" appears). The church and the Community Club look the same, and the center of town looks the same, although recently a small store attached to the post office has begun selling coffee and pastries on the weekend. Outside the immediate circumference of the center of Brookside, McMansions have arisen on what had been the Bockoven dairy farm and in the area bordering Mt. Freedom that was, relatively speaking, the poorest section of the town, called unfortunately in my home the "redneck" section. Some of the least expensive homes in Brookside also neighbored Bockoven's farm. No one with enough money wanted to smell cow shit. A small monument built from the stones of the barn has been placed on the

Bockoven Dairy Farm historical marker. Alan Edelson, HMdb.org.

location of the barn. It reads: "This stone monument was constructed from a foundation of a barn on the former Bockoven farm. This was the site of the last working dairy farm in Brookside." High above this monument on the fields of this old dairy farm in the pastures above the barn, where the cows once grazed, is now a small herd of McMansions circa $1,000,000 apiece in price.

The Pitney Farm was an expansive farm and estate of over 200 acres near the center of Brookside dating back to 1722 when James Pitney, an Englishman, bought land east of Mendham, and it remained in the Pitney family into the twenty-first century, although in the mid-twentieth century the family began selling off some of the lands that became housing developments alongside lands that became homes near the center of town in Harmony Acres, Hilltop Circle, Knollwood Trail, and Butternut Drive. In 2009, the remaining twelve acres of Pitney Farm were purchased by Mendham Township with a combination of $1.5 million in Morris County Open Space funds and township funds. Seven acres of this farm have now become the Historic Park at Pitney Farm. Mendham Township is continuing its efforts to secure funds from the New Jersey Department of Environmental Protection Green Acres Program for a stewardship grant and from the Morris County Trail Construction Grant Program for the park. Five acres were auctioned off to a developer and debates continue about the development and the shape of the preservation and use of this land.[3]

Brookside had begun sorting itself out in the mid-twentieth century into a more homogenous place by class through the regulations of exclusionary zoning that eventually led to the creation of what Linda Prevost has called "snob zones."[4] In New Jersey, the diaspora from Newark of whites and white ethnics and Jews moving up and out to the suburbs transformed a Newark from a white population of 89 percent in 1940 to 44 percent in 1970 and a non-white population of 11 percent in 1940 to 55 percent in 1970, with the 1967 riot becoming the catalyst for a redistribution of Newark's white population—and that of Paterson and Jersey City too—to the suburban periphery, with Swede escaping further out into the country than many.[5] In an interview for the *Newark News* in 1958 on the event of his publication of *Goodbye, Columbus*, Roth explained, "My work concerns the geographical dispersion of Jews, what happens when they move from Prince Street to West Orange—it really is the story of immigrant to 'nouveau rich.'"[6] Roth, it appears, at the time of this interview, envisioned his own future as part of this dispersion, as his interviewer ends his story concluding, "He is enamored enough with New Jersey to want to live in the suburbs—'preferably Glen Ridge' [a suburb of Newark not far from West Orange or Short Hills]—when he gives up bachelorhood."[7] The Patimkins themselves in

Goodbye, Columbus are able, unlike Roth's own family, to move to the suburbs and are part of a generation that left Newark and who, in Roth's words, "moved further and further west.... up the slope of the Orange Mountains, until they had reached the crest and started down the other side, pouring into Gentile territory as the Scotch-Irish had poured through the Cumberland Gap."[8] Roth makes the Jewish diaspora from Newark a vital theme for his literature of the Garden State, with Swede Levov as one of these exiles and pioneers, heading further west into gentile territory.

Newark became a large majority of one minority in terms of race and class—a Black, lower-class minority—while at the receiving end of the diaspora, places in western Morris County such as Mendham Township experienced a sorting out that homogenized itself mostly along upper-middle-class and upper-class lines (and whiteness). Formerly, in the 1960s on West Main Street, set between the post office in the center of town and the entrance to Mendham Township Elementary School and neighboring the home of Morris Frank, the most famous person in the town—a blind man who was the founder of the Seeing Eye—was the home of Miss Margaret O'Brian, the "cat lady" (so called by kids). Her home was a Halloween house of horror 365 days of the year: a scary, almost haunted place—a dilapidated home with dead cats on the porch to be seen by those of us who dared to walk up to the front door and look in for the fright of it. She would commute from her home in Brookside to her job at a fine linen store in Morristown in a car from the 1930s, driving slowly on its balloonish tires, building up long lines of cars behind her. When she died, the house was torn down with its land bought by the Franks. As more wealth moved in, other old homes in Brookside were razed, with McMansions sprouting up in their place like mushrooms. One old, unpainted, derelict home off Cherry Lane within a stone's throw of the municipal building was the home of the Hazards (a family of three sisters, Sallie, Margaret, and Abigail, and a brother, Tommy) who kept a small goat farm of maybe five to seven goats in the backyard. The home had dirt floors and goats could be seen wandering into it. This too was torn down and the land became part of a small housing development of several homes on Butternut Drive that includes the one where Steven Cramer would live in the late 1960s.

12. Brookside Bards: Steven Cramer's Poetry of Protest and Christopher Merrill's Poetry of Place

Steven Cramer's poem "The Parade, 1968" appeared in his first collection of poems, *The World Book*. His second collection of poems is called *Goodbye to the Orchard*.[1] Three of the poems in his first two collections offer a poetry of place about Brookside that also contains riffs of protest, which make them more of a good riddance than a goodbye to the orchard (or even something of a fuck you verbal bomb to the "orchard," not totally dissimilar in spirit from Merry's bombing of the Old Rimrock post office). "The Battle of the Bands" features a band composed of Brookside teenagers performing that includes Fred Hartley, the son of Al and Hermine Hartley, who is in the photo used on the original cover of *American Pastoral*. Fred is described "thumbing his Fender bass, adorably saurian / In thigh-tight Naugahyde."[2] He is now the pastor of One Mission Church (formerly Lilburn Alliance) in Georgia and leader of College of Prayer International. Another member of this band, Ken Lurie, who also participated in the 1969 Fourth of July parade protest, is now a retired professor from the music department at Appalachian State University. Another poem in this collection that draws on the area is "For the Bullies of West Morris High." In *American Pastoral*, Merry Levov attends Morristown High School, but the high school for students from Brookside in the 1960s was West Morris Regional. Cramer's poem gives expression to the dissent we can hear in Merry Levov of a teenager not fitting into a suburban social circle subject to mockery and bullying, a dissent against a discomfort that is more typical than unique for so many teenagers, and at West Morris was exacerbated by another difference: beyond the Mendhams and in the territories closer to the high school—Chester, Long Valley, Flanders, Schooley's Mountain—it was no longer the territory of white-collar commuters to New York City. Cramer's most effective poem of protest remains "The Parade, 1968."

Cramer's second collection of poems, *Goodbye to the Orchard*, strikes a resonant note in its title when juxtaposed against Philip Roth's literature of New Jersey beginning with *Goodbye, Columbus*. Steven Cramer became part of a diaspora in a different direction: children who grew up in Brookside but then said goodbye to the orchard and gave a welcome to big city life as Merry Levov wants to do as well. This diaspora in reverse is unlimned in most literature, while the diaspora of "white ethnics" from a city—a Newark or East Orange—to the suburbs is so often the story of Roth's fiction from *Goodbye, Columbus* to *American Pastoral* (as it is part of the story of *The*

Sopranos and the life of Chris Christie). The Newark of Roth's childhood (and of Amiri Baraka)—was a Newark, in Roth's words, of a "majority composed of the competing minorities," a babel of voices not just of different ethnicities but different social classes and religions—that sorted itself by choice and circumstance (RMO, p. 107). The circumstances that confined the choices included the exclusionary zoning of the suburbs, with their policies of minimum lot sizes for the orchards and farmland sold off and developed into housing subdivisions. Newark became a large majority of one minority in terms of race and class—a Black, mostly lower-class minority—while at the receiving end of the diaspora, places in western Morris County such as Mendham Township experienced their own sorting out. As the nouveau riche moved in, lower-class white families were priced out. Again, the broken down, unpainted, home of the Hazards, with goats in the backyard just off Cherry Lane and very close to the center of town, was torn down and the land sold off for a small housing development of a few homes that included again the one where Steven Cramer lived. The poems of his *Goodbye to the Orchard* are the lyrics from a diaspora in reverse—the desire to leave the garden world for the city or a somewhere else—a desire and ambition articulated in the screams by Merry Levov as well as to my ear in the verse of Cramer.

Christopher Merrill in the second poem in *Workbook* entitled "Poaching" also addresses the protest against the Vietnam War at Brookside's Fourth of July parade in 1969. He writes, "But here invention flags before the facts: / When Sam Tufts (volunteer fire chief, Babe Ruth / Team coach, and plumber) choked a black-robed boy / One Fourth of July, honoring the way / In Asia and the memory of his nephew—/ Fergus' son—by protesting the students' / protest of our parade (their coffin lay / In pieces near the judges' stand), the sun / Burned through the fittings in the clouds, and burst / Into the students' song."[3] Philip Roth writes that history twice erupted in Old Rimrock in ways that shook America beyond its own walls: George Washington and the Revolutionary War and Merry Levov's bomb exploding in the post office. The name of Corporal Robert Bruce Tufts (Fergus's son) on the monument just across the street from the post office reminds me indelibly how history in the form of the violence of the Vietnam War struck one family in a more devastating way than probably even the Levovs are affected by Merry Levov's bomb. Christopher Merrill has now supplemented his poems set in Brookside with a memoir, *Self-Portrait with Dogwood*, in which he tells compelling stories of his own memories of Brookside including the protest at the 1969 Fourth of July parade and a wonderful account of the legend of Tempe Wick whose story was first told by Frank R. Stockton in 1896.[4] He also tells the haunting story of a mutual friend and classmate at the Pingry School—a private high school in Hillside near its border with Elizabeth that we both attended—from Brookside and his decline into mental illness during his high school years in an act of self-mutilation under drugs that devasted his family and offers, if you will, a nonfictional complement and implosion to the anti-pastoral trajectory of Merry Levov.[5]

Without asking, and whatever our differences are about the Brookside of our coming of age, I am rather certain Steven Cramer, a classmate of mine in seventh and eighth grade, and Christopher Merrill, a next-door neighbor of mine for a year or two, would agree with me: Roth has

War memorial with Vietnam plaque in front of Mendham Township municipal building. (Photo by Thomas Gustafson.)

created a remarkable novel in its own sense of place and in its own complex protest that makes us feel that in 1968 Swede could be our neighbor and, even more, Merry our classmate.

For the Fourth of July parade in 2012, the town took for its theme the 1960s, calling it a day when Brookside would become Brookstock. There were no coffins in that parade that reminded people of the death of Robert Tufts or any of the 58,000 Americans killed in the Vietnam War or of a death of social conscience. The poetry of Steven Cramer and Christopher Merrill and *American Pastoral* are means for us not to forget how torn up a small town like Brookside and America itself became over the Vietnam War. A visit to the encampment of the Continental army in Jockey Hollow becomes a means for us as well to remember the sacrifices made and the hardship for the soldiers of the Revolutionary War. But mostly when students go there on field trips, as I did in elementary school and on other occasions, it was a place for us kids to play soldier. The violence of the Revolutionary War tends to be forgotten like the violence of the Vietnam War during a Brookstock parade or 1960s theme party. I daresay the scars inside of kids bullied in Brookside and at West Morris High School—and at Morristown High School—on the basis of race or religion or looks or any other basis are maybe even harder to forget for them than the tragedies of the Vietnam War . . . unless you are a child of Fergus or Sam Tufts.

Part III

Pentecost Remembered and Lost

● ● ● ● ● ● ● ● ● ●

13. Brookside against the Current

Brookside cherishes the illusion of its historylessness, its immunity from history. Its Main Street world, anchored by its post office and the Community Club, has changed less than Disneyland's Main Street since the 1950s. The main things that Brookside has added over the last fifty years is one new baseball field, an addition to the municipal building that is hidden in back, hundreds of acres of more park space, and some markers for Patriot's Path, and the two names added to its memorial for people from Brookside who died serving in war: Corporal Robert Bruce Tufts and John T. Glanville Jr., lieutenant commander, US Navy, in the Vietnam War. The building between the post office and the Congregational church that served as a bank branch for a time in the 1960s has been bought by the church and refit. It serves no commercial function. Brookside is where people came for a green world, and those who did come here from somewhere have succeeded, by and large, in doing this. To afford a place here now, you have to be a success. This was a place, unlike Bernardsville or Far Hills, not of old money but new money. There was some old money here, such as the nine generations of the Pitney estate. But the Orcutts were few. They lived elsewhere. The whiteness of Brookside as well as the wealth of its new generations of residents fostered this illusion. No one seemed to be held down by their ethnicity. No one appeared to be reminded of limitation because of their color in the 1960s (as the place had almost no people of color). This was the promise of America as Crèvecoeur most famously described it his third letter in *Letters from an America Farmer.*[1] Crèvecoeur writes of slavery in other letters in this book, but so often his letter about slavery in the South is not anthologized. This was Brookside. The whiteness of it all—and the new money of it all—rendered history too invisible.

Brookside in the 1960s was a place shaped by the force of preserving a place zoned to be idyllic. It was also a place devoted to protecting itself from a future or the dynamic that transforms almost every other place: the demographic change that comes with affordable housing. The trajectory seems inevitable: the green world of open space becomes the farm and then the farm becomes the suburb and then the suburb becomes the city. The pastoral gets transformed by success. The success—or the allure—of Brookside, in contrast, was at once in being a place where one could escape the past and escape the future. Brookside, unlike Newark, and unlike Mendham Borough, would not change. It would not bring in business and it has resisted zoning and approving construction for affordable housing in the form of rental apartments or even condos. The wealth of the town enabled it to free itself from what cursed Mendham Borough in the view of some Brooksiders: they did not need or desire commercial development to lower taxes, and they tapped into the tax money from the state designated for conservation funds to create parks and preserve open space (and preserve or increase the value of their homes). Brookside expanded its garden and extended its guardian walls with green money: property taxes and Green Acres funds. Swede Levov could see and feel the allure of such a place. It is the same allure that Nathan Zuckerman in Roth's *The Counterlife* ascribes to a certain vision for Israel. Nathan's brother Henry flees from New Jersey in this novel to the Jewish settlement of Agor in Israel:

> As I discovered at Agor, not even Jews, who are to history what Eskimos are to snow, seem able, despite the arduous education to the contrary, to protect themselves against the pastoral myth of life before Cain and Abel, of life before the split began. Fleeing now, and back to day zero and the first untainted settlement—breaking history's mold and casting off the dirty, disfiguring reality of the piled-up years: this is what Judea means to, of all people, that belligerent, unillusioned little band of Jews. . . . the idyllic scenario of redemption through the recovery of a sanitized, confusionless life. In dead seriousness, we all create imagined worlds, often green and breastlike, where we may finally be "ourselves." (C, p. 322)

There is no better update of Crèvecoeur's dream of America as a new world; there is no better articulation of what Seymour sees in Old Rimrock. Against the current of history, Brookside preserves for the future a past that never

was, clamoring in harmony to seal the garden against a berserk outside of its walls and "satanic" industry within its
own past.

Brookside, in its myths, is not founded on a fratricide
or rape or conquest, like Rome or frontier towns of the
American West. But it does have a history of a split
between Cain and Abel, not a deadly one, just a division.
Mendham Borough and Mendham Township split apart
from each other. Mendham Borough went in the direction
of more commercial development. Mendham Township
defined itself as the un-Mendham as well as the non-
Newark. It would be a place of no satanic mills, no industry, no glove factories, not even the business of a grocery
store or a pharmacy. That was for Mendham, not Brookside. Brookside would go more green, more pastoral, not
less, and it would do this through the zoning ordinances
that ruled out commerce and through wetlands protection
activism and the delaying tactics of legal proceedings that
resisted rental apartments and condominiums (except for
doctors' offices and one other hidden exception: the Mendham Golf & Tennis Club could sell golf balls and other
equipment for golf and tennis). The illusion is that free
from the transforming forces of history—the history that
transformed Paterson and Newark and that began turning every garden space in the Garden State into a paved
paradise—Brookside kept reversing history, turning more
and more of its space into park space, open space. As it
began protecting more and more of its space, and as some
of its recreational hunters left town, unable to afford it,
moving to Hunterdon County or eastern Pennsylvania,
one problem that Brookside began to face was too many
deer: deer eating the vegetation of backyard flower gardens, deer spreading Lyme disease, deer being a danger on

the roads. Brookside was not haunted by the specter of violent crime; it became haunted by Lyme disease and deer jumping in front of cars, causing accidents. In Brookside, in the twenty-first century, there appears to be now more deer and wildlife, including foxes, pheasants, and turkeys, in backyards than in the 1960s.

But deep down, Old Rimrock was for Swede Levov akin to this new Israel that Henry Zuckerman seeks in Agor: a place where one could be freed from the oppressions of history and from persecution because of one's religion. This would also be an idyllic place that retained a sense of community. Brookside had a community life, the Community Club, a community Fourth of July parade, a civic life (and, unlike Morristown, schools with a good reputation). The post office here, in this regard, was something of a kibbutz room. Brookside was a place of talk, of gossip, a social place. Classical political philosophers would argue that for democracy to thrive in a polis, the polis could not become too big, too large. The 3,500 people of Mendham Township in the 1960s were spread out, miles from each other, in three separate neighborhoods, but within Mendham Township, Brookside was a smaller place, with a stronger sense of community in part because of that post office and because it was the government center of the town, the home of its central crossroads and its school. In Brookside, three streams converged, two from the north and one from the west. Brookside was something of a Pittsburgh in this regard, a three rivers place, with its first little industries dependent on these three rivers. The industries left. The farms left. But what Brookside prided itself on retaining was not just a sense of freedom defined as an escape from the city, but a sense of community even if complete with its malcontents.

Swede Levov imagines Old Rimrock as a place where he would not face resentment. His origin and his religion would not be held against him. Racial prejudice was not palpable as an obstacle because the place was so racially homogeneous. Racism of course was there in Brookside, but it was directed outside in the direction of Black Newark and brown Dover and even at a more Italian Mendham. Merry Levov concludes from her experience in Old Rimrock that "there could never be a revolution in America to uproot the forces of racism and reaction and greed" (p. 260). Brookside or Old Rimrock can serve as a symbol of this as much as, if not more than, Newark. Brookside is at once the flight from what Newark—and even Morristown and Mt. Freedom and Dover—represented and a passive aggressive fight against it fought on the almost invisible battlefield of zoning regulation. The term "open space" to designate the many acres (3,000-plus of the township's 11,000) preserved from development as designated by the green spaces on Mendham Township's preserved and institutional lands map can be regarded as a euphemism for "closed-off" space.

Democracy demands that we turn our anger into battles of words in the forum, not fights with bombs and Molotov cocktails, but American democracy has sanctioned its share of wars and bombings. It began with a war—the Revolution—fought more in New Jersey than any other state. Merry thinks of herself as the "Joan of Arc of the movement" according to Nathan Zuckerman (p. 160). She locates her own self in a more American tradition, explaining to her father, "The disobedience of oppressive laws.... including violent disobedience, goes back to abolitionism," and Nathan adds, "his daughter is one with John Brown!" (p. 160). Roth locates it in Morristown and the Revolution.

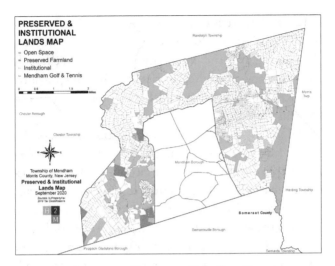

Preserved and institutional lands map of Mendham Township, 2020.
Mendham Township.

"So we beat on, boats against the current, borne back
ceaselessly into the past."[2] This sentence, which concludes
The Great Gatsby, remains one of the most significant concluding lines of any work of American literature, matched
up with Huck Finn's resolution at the end of *The Adventures of Huckleberry Finn* to "light out for the territory."[3]
But just as significant is the ending of Ralph Ellison's *Invisible Man* where we find the Invisible Man, at the end of
the novel, in a basement, tapping into the electricity of the
power company to illuminate the darkness and his invisibility. That ending, of course, is a parable about Ellison's
effort, which is the effort of Roth and so many American
writers, to tap into the power of words to illuminate our
places of darkness, beginning with the original sins in this
New World of genocide and ethnic cleansing against
American Indians and the enslavement of people from

Africa and of African descent. *American Pastoral* celebrates the lighting out for the territory, but it also celebrates the lighting up—the illumination—of a place through its history and through its stories (but the ones provided by Lou and Jerry Levov and Bucky more than Swede and Bill Orcutt).

Ralph Ellison has written two collections of essays, the first called *Shadow and Act* and the other *Going to the Territory*, that offer an incisive perspective on American literature in its political and cultural contexts. Ellison writes in *Going to the Territory*, "In the beginning of America was not only the word but the contradiction of the word," and in *Shadow and Act*, "For if the word has the potency to revive and make us free, it has also the power to blind, imprison, and destroy."[4] Tony Kushner writes in another great essay, "American Things," about how the "frazzle" of dissonance is part of our movement forward, and it is this dissonance and its interplay with consensus—so beautifully heard in the interplay between the lyrical and cacophonous sounds in Jimi Hendrix's version of the "Star-Spangled Banner"—that Roth helps us hear more clearly in *American Pastoral*: the cacophony of the dinner party conversation in the "Paradise Lost" section, but also the point and counterpoint of the debates between Merry and her grandfather, Lou, and between Swede and his daughter in Newark, and the point-counterpoint of the two histories of Morris County offered by Bill Orcutt and by Bucky Robinson.[5] This is the dissonance, the contradiction, the debate necessary to hear so as to understand the history of Brookside and Old Rimrock and any American town or state and the country itself. Merry can hear the dissonant chords, the frazzle, of Hendrix's "Star-Spangled Banner," while her father, Swede, in effect, attunes his ear to the lyricism of Hendrix's version of the song as it aspires to rise above the cacophony—the sounds of sirens and machine guns and bombs and riot.

American Pastoral itself has the same lyricism of Hendrix's "Star-Spangled Banner" aspiring to rise above the cacophony, the babel, the frazzle of discord. Roth represents for us such a moment of discord overcome in the conversation between Lou Levov and Jim Dwyer about the Newark and Elizabeth of their childhood memories. But fortunately, Hendrix's music and *American Pastoral* and Martin Luther King Jr.'s "I Have a Dream" speech, for all their gospel aspiration to overcome the blues and overcome the dissonance of the American past, remind us of that discord in lyrical and dramatic ways. The song we too often want to hear in America is not the song with the dissonance in it of Hendrix's "Star-Spangled Banner" or "Trouble Every Day" (also known as the Watts Riot song) by Frank Zappa and the Mothers of Invention, but a song that has the sound that President Ronald Reagan's celebrates as the "American sound" at the end of his second inaugural address: This song is "hopeful, big-hearted, idealistic, daring, decent and fair."[6] These are lines that would make a Merry Levov berserk, or that would make her want to throw verbal bombs at this sentimental, nostalgic, fairy tale that is American patriotic mythology. The United States (until Juneteenth) did not have a holiday in the spirit of the Jewish holiday of Yom Kippur that calls on people to reflect on the past not in prideful self-congratulation but humility and apology (although such a holiday would certainly be transformed, as Sacvan Bercovitch's scholarship forecasts, into a jeremiad that would serve to celebrate America and its errand and its sense of place as a promised land).[7] Most Brooksiders denounced the coffin at the end of the Fourth of July parade in 1969, and such a holiday would put a coffin for deaths of the Pequot massacre, the Salem witch executions, the Middle Passage, lynchings, pogroms, wars for empire, and so on, at the beginning of the parade rather than words from John Winthrop about "a city on a hill" or words from the Declaration of Independence about "all men are created equal."

14. NIMBY: Protecting Green Space with Green Money

Nowhere is there a new colony—however utopian the desires of its founders may be—where there can be no prison, claims Nathaniel Hawthorne in the opening of *The Scarlet Letter*. Brookside fought hard to be an exception to this claim when its greenness—its pastoralism—was threatened by the blackness of a proposed prison site. Morristown is the county seat and the location of the courthouse and jail for Morris County. When the county planned in the early 1990s to build a new prison in Morris Township on the border between Morristown and Mendham Township off Prudence Lane in the Washington Valley area of Mendham Township, NIMBYism—not in my backyard—stirred residents (including my father and mother, whose home was then on Prudence Lane) into protest. Thanks to this chorus of NIMBY protests, the prison site was relocated to a neighborhood in the city of Morristown that was primarily African American in the 1960s and is now more Latino. This threat of a prison adjoining the Washington Valley area of Mendham Township also led to a successful effort to register Washington Valley in 1992 as a historic district with the National Park

Service's National Register of Historic Places, a federal government program that began in 1966 to coordinate and support public and private efforts to identify, evaluate, and protect historic places worthy of preservation. The NIMBY opposition to the jail site also helped lead Mendham Township to create the Mendham Township Historic Preservation Committee in 1991, which has now succeeded in creating five historic district neighborhoods in Mendham Township registered with the Department of the Interior: Washington Valley (1992), Brookside (1995), Combs Hollow (1995), Ralston (1997), and Tempe Wick (2000). The claims of historic preservation now combine even more strongly with the claims of environmental protection and wetlands ordinances as a means to protect the "garden" of Mendham Township.[1]

Swede Levov imagines himself as Johnny Appleseed in a garden world as he walks from his home to the center of Old Rimrock to pick up a paper at the post office, but he seems innocent about all the forces—the politics, the lobbying, the wealth, the pulling of strings, and so on—that conspired to create this green world. Later participating in a controversy over the Morris County jail in one of his own first political battles was Chris Christie when he was serving his first term as a freeholder for Morris County (1995–1998). He made comments about the architect of the prison that led to a suit against him for defamation.[2] When Christie ran for a second term as freeholder, he campaigned in part on how he helped reduce taxes in Morris County. But Christie also voted to raise the county's "open space tax" that generated money for land preservation.[3] Time and again in Mendham Township, open space such as the green world that Swede enjoys in Old Rimrock was preserved thanks to the town and its homeowner activists

gaining funds from places such the New Jersey Conservation Foundation and from the Department of Housing
and Urban Development (HUD). HUD was founded in
1965 as part of LBJ's Great Society programs. Its mission
is to create strong, sustainable, inclusive communities
free from discrimination. Somehow Mendham Township tapped into its funds to help preserve open space for
one of the wealthiest and most unaffordable—and least
diverse—places in New Jersey. This part of Morris County's most successful act of NIMBY protest was its resistance
beginning in 1959 to the location of a new major airport
in the Great Swamp area (in the New Providence area).[4]
Protests and NIMBY opposition in Mendham Township
later successfully opposed plans AT&T had to use land
they purchased from the Boy Scouts of America—the
Schiff Scout Reservation—for a training facility. Facing
this resistance, AT&T sold this land to a developer. The
town initially resisted efforts to develop this land, and
thanks in part to this resistance, a compromise was
reached: 700 acres were set aside as the Schiff Nature Preserve and 100-plus acres of the land became an exclusive
development of eighty-five single-family homes called
Brookrace.

Resistance to development is in the DNA or origin
story of Mendham Township and its split off from Mendham Borough into Mendham Township in 1906 when
some residents wanted to fund the creation of a public
water and sewage system and some did not. The side that
wanted the infrastructure improvements became Mendham Borough, and the side that refused became Mendham
Township, a difference that would persist as Mendham
Township set itself up to be the non–Mendham Borough,
resisting the lure of bringing in commercial development

to lower taxes. Mendham Township had the money, the power, the interest, and the desire to keep itself as it was, and today the center of Brookside is less commercial than it was in the past, with one of the buildings in the very small commercial zone now owned by the Congregational church, and the post office—which had been a general store until the early 1960s—now solely a post office, with an attached side building now a gift and knickknack store that sells coffee on the weekends. The one house near the center of town in the commercial district that carried on a small business in the back for designing and sewing and selling women's sports clothing no longer contains a space for any commercial activity. Unlike neighboring Mendham and Morris Township, the two public places to swim maintained by the recreation department for Mendham Township are both ponds (the one near the center of town, next to the elementary school, is called Brookside Beach). Again, one significant change in the town is the increase in size of the police force from a department of two officers in the 1960s to fifteen currently, a ratio of police to population (1:350) that exceeds that of Los Angeles (1:420).

The advocates of the pastoral in Mendham Township have kept from its environs a jail and almost all commerce, but every garden world has its walls and boundaries and defenses, however hidden, however invisible. Lou Levov, commenting on the fall of Newark in his lifetime when everything has been ripped off or ripped up, including the cobblestones from the streets, remarks "But, mark my words, Newark will be the city that never comes back" (p. 345). Mark my words, Brookside will be the town that never goes forward in commercial development. But an annual event that has now taken place at the Brookside Beach in the summer since 2021 demands that I must bite my Lou Levov tongue about Brookside never going forward in an embrace of diversity and the multiculturalism of the twenty-first century. Brookside Beach has become the setting for an "annual Pride movie night" sponsored by the Mendhams Stigma-Free Task Force, the Brookside Community Church, the Mendham Diversity Committee, and EdgeNJ, a Denville-based nonprofit that provides support and wellness services to the LGBTQ community.[5]

15. The Price of Harmony

Mark Shechner argues that *American Pastoral* "possesses a brawling, rambunctious, quarrelsome, kvetching magnificence," and that is so anti-pastoral and so un-Brookside.[1] The conversational style of Brookside is pleasantry. Frankness—pointedness—is saved for gossip. The style seems not learned, not taught, not imitated, just absorbed. But it is taught through the look of the eye, the raised eyebrow, the reminders to say thank you. The antithesis of this polite style is the hardscrabble, in your face, tell it like it is, inelegant, vulgar brashness of a Chris Christie that New Jersey is as famous for as its toxic dumps. Brooksiders like my mom would have one curt line to put Christie in his place: he's Newark. Whitney Houston, from Newark, on the other hand, charmed Mendham Township for a time. She needed the cooperation of the town services for certain additions to her home in the exclusive Oak Knoll neighborhood of Ralston and of the police for her wedding to Bobby Brown that she held at her home, and she thanked the town by inviting some of its officials to her wedding. It was an A-list party with township officials delighting conspicuously in an invite to it, a contrast to the fears so many had in 1967, from the police chief and the fire chief on down, about African Americans coming out from Newark to bring the riot to Brookside. Green power—money—and fame got Houston her pass from Newark to Brookside, just as money got the pass from Newark to Brookside for Otto Badenhausen and for Chris Christie and for Swede from Newark to Old Rimrock.

There is circumspection to this suburban style. Audrey Hepburn, the former idol of Merry before her embrace of the Weathermen, not Chris Christie, not Whitney Houston, would be its preferred icon. This circumspection is what Nathan Zuckerman in *The Counterlife* would call "circumcision": a cutting off of the natural (C, p. 323). Jerry Levov, not Swede, is the voice of the natural, lamenting in lambasts of Swede the decision of his brother to move to Old Rimrock: "Out there with Miss America, dumbing down and dulling out. Out there playing at being Wasps, a little Mick girl from the Elizabeth docks and a Jewboy from Weequahic High. The cows. Cow society. Colonial old America. And you thought all that façade was going to come without cost. Genteel and innocent. *But that costs, too, Seymour. I* would have thrown a bomb. *I* would become a Jain and live in Newark. That Wasp bullshit!" (AP, p. 280). Nathan Zuckerman in *The Counterlife* upbraids himself in a similar way for desiring at once a place and an art of "tranquility." "But tranquility is disquieting to you, Nathan, in writing particularly—it's bad art to you, far too comfortable for the reader and certainly for yourself" (C, p. 317). He adds, "The last thing you want is to make readers happy, with everything cozy and strifeless, and desire simply fulfilled. The pastoral is not your genre, and Zuckerman Domesticus now seems to you just that, too easy a

solution, an idyll of the kind you hate, a fantasy of innocence in the perfect house in the perfect landscape on the
banks of the perfect stretch of river" (C, p. 317).

Swede transforms himself into this counterimage of
Zuckerman: "Zuckerman Domesticus." Old Rimrock
for him as a place will be what the genre of pastoral is
for Zuckerman: "strifeless," "an idyll," "tranquility." For
Merry, like for Jerry, the place is "Wasp bullshit," but
Merry does not just hurl verbal bombs of obscenity against
an Old Rimrock as an incarnation of the American "civil
religion" betrayed: she bombs the place. For me that bomb
is in part a bomb against what the politeness can never
hide: the vulgarity of wealth, the vulgarity of prejudice, the
vulgarity of a contentment purchased at a cost that we here
who live in Brookside are not Mendham Borough, and
certainly not Mt. Freedom, and even more certainly not
Newark. Merry, like Thomas Jefferson, John Adams, Nat
Turner, John Brown, is the word and act of dissent turned
violent. Swede Levov, like Ben Franklin in his *Autobiography* and the founding fathers on the issue of slavery in
Philadelphia in 1787 and Booker T. Washington in his
Atlanta Address of 1895 and Ronald Reagan in his campaign for governor in 1965 countering the Free Speech
Movement at Berkeley and voicing opposition to the civil
rights legislation of 1965, is the word and action of a dissent repressed in favor of a compromised harmony that has
its costs, as Jerry Levov understands.

Zuckerman in *The Counterlife* expounds further on
the pastoral, explaining that the genre begins in "those
irrepressible yearnings by people beyond simplicity to be
taken off to the perfectly safe, charmingly simple and sat-
isfying environment that is desire's homeland. How moving and pathetic these pastorals are that cannot admit

contradiction or conflict!" (C, p. 322). He adds that "at the core" of pastoral is "the idyllic scenario of redemption through the recovery of a sanitized, confusionless life. In dead seriousness, we all create imagined worlds, often green and breastlike, where we may finally be 'ourselves'" (C, p. 322). Roth's *American Pastoral* admits contradiction and conflict. Its style, its narrative of conflict, its babel of tongues, the stuttering and the silence of Merry Levov, and her striking out with a bombing, like Billy Budd's death strike against John Claggart in *Billy Budd*, undermine Swede's desire for the pastoral as much as the conclusion of Melville's *Billy Budd* undermines Captain Vere's belief that "forms, measured forms, are everything," the "import," in Vere's reading, of the "story of Orpheus, with his lyre spellbinding the wild denizens of the wood," which Vere applies "to the disruption of forms going on across the Channel and the consequences thereof."[2] Billy Budd, like Merry (and Billy Budd's fellow sailors), are breachers of decorum; their allegiance is not to an enforced silence on board a warship, be it the *Bellipotent* under the command of Vere or America at war in Vietnam under the command of Lyndon Baines Johnson or Richard Nixon. Melville's allegiance, however sympathetically he portrays Captain Vere, appears to be to the *Rights of Man* and the spirit of 1776, the year Billy Budd was born, the year Paine pens *Common Sense*, the year Jefferson drafts the Declaration of Independence, his justification for going to war against England in part because the King of England had been "deaf to the voice of justice & consanguinity."[3] Merry pledges that same allegiance with her bomb. Roth gives us the conflict, the contradiction: Swede's aspiration for the pastoral (departing Newark for Old Rimrock) versus his daughter's aspiration for the anti-pastoral (escaping Old Rimrock for visits to New York) is a conflict that recapitulates the debate over remaining loyal to the king in 1776 and the debate over harmonizing with the founding fathers on slavery in antebellum America versus starting up a slave rebellion as did Nat Turner and John Brown. The pastoral life of the Swede in Old Rimrock is not reprehensible, or it is by no means as reprehensible as harmonizing with injustice for the sake of safety and security, but it has its price, an expensive price: the dysfunction, the dissonance, of his family as Swede's own triumphs seem to tune him out too much both to the sufferings that disturb his daughter and to the bigotries of intolerance in Old Rimrock and its environs that his brother Jerry never forgets.[4]

Swede Levov's embrace of the ideal of a rural retreat, which finds its incarnation in Old Rimrock, has a deep history stretching back in American culture to Thomas Jefferson's agrarian ideal and long before that in Western culture to the pastoral visions of Virgil and Hesiod and their longing for a world elsewhere far from the motley of the marketplace as well as from the battlefield and the corruptions of a court world. Now in America that pastoral ideal has migrated from the heartland of a farm or the ranch to the preserve of the country estate and to those other more nouveau riche forms of the suburban enclave and the gated subdivision, places walled off from the congestion, the crowdedness, the heterogeneity, and the "berserkness" of the urban crucible. The price paid for walling off garden worlds from what is fallen outside its boundaries—be it the noise and smells and smog of the industrial city or crime and violence or all the bustle and billboards of commercial activity—can create, it seems, a ledger of emotional deficit that cannot be balanced: the dissents and disturbances of a Merry Levov and the denials of a Swede Levov who aspires to transcend the history of a place built on exclusive restrictions against all that is not as white or as wealthy as Swede or as green as a golf course or that is as unharmonious as radical protest against a real American berserk that goes about its errands all too normally—its racism, antisemitism, greed, violence.

Nathan Zuckerman claims in *The Counterlife* that the "pastoral stops here and it stops with circumcision" (C, p. 323). "Circumcision," he explains, "is everything that the pastoral is not and, to my mind, reinforces what the world is about, which isn't strifeless unity. Quite convincingly, circumcision gives the lie to the womb-dream of life in the beautiful state of innocent prehistory, the appealing idyll of living 'naturally,' unencumbered by man-made ritual. To be born is to lose all that. The heavy hand of human values falls upon you right at the start, marking your genitals as its own" (C, p. 323). But part of the mark that American culture leaves on us is the circle of its words, the words of its "civil religion," its logos, its logocracy. These circles of words can be read to celebrate both the joy of remaining protected within its rings, including the circle of words that are the Bill of Rights, and also the joy, the need, the necessity of breaking out of these circles to pursue liberty, or a more perfect union, or a world that is more fresh, more green, more just. That breaking away from any circle or city of words—as well as living immersed in words and talk and conversation and the rich babel of tongues that is America—is what Emerson celebrates in his essay "Circles." Roth celebrates this too in *American Pastoral*, when he gives us, in the third part of the novel called "Paradise Lost," a respite from the fallen world of babel that is the dinner party hosted by the Levovs. Zuckerman offers in counterpoint the remembrance of a Pentecostal moment in the past, before the 1960s: the Thanksgiving table at the Levovs when the two patriarchs, Lou Levov and Jim Dwyer, converge in communion as they share together stories of their almost common, neighboring ground of their hometowns, Newark and Elizabeth.

16. The Table of Otherhood and Communion

A dream vision of America—and the dream of Swede Levov for life in Old Rimrock—is e pluribus unum. This dream is best figured through two metaphors that Martin Luther King Jr. calls on in his "I Have a Dream" speech: the dream of overcoming our divisions to unite in singing one song and sitting down together at a table of brotherhood. Let us "transform the jangling discords of our nation into a beautiful symphony of brotherhood."[1] These two figurations of the dream are deeply rooted in the American dream, going back to a vision of communion through an embrace of the word of God articulated by John Winthrop in his "Model of Christian Charity" and the iconic act of communion through the breaking of bread between pilgrim and American Indian of the Thanksgiving story. Each metaphor has its biblical origin—the Babel story of Genesis and the Last Supper of the New Testament—and each is part of a tradition that Roth riffs on in *American Pastoral*. In the beginning, the "whole earth was of one language, and of one speech" (Genesis 11:1). But God, in order to punish the excessive pride of man in building a tower to scale the heavens, visits on the people a confusion of tongues. "Because the lord did there confound the language of all the earth; and from thence did the Lord scatter them abroad the face of all the earth" (Genesis 11: 7–8). The Tower of Babel, however, is not the last chapter in the biblical history of language. After Christ's crucifixion, in the revelation of Pentecost, the Holy Spirit descends on the apostles and gives them the gift of tongues: "And there appeared to them tongues as of fire, distributed and resting on each of them" (Acts 2:3). The dispersal into multiplicity is compensated for by a miraculous gift for recovering the communion of a scattered, diverse people.

Just as biblical history gives us the story of a people falling into the confusion of Babel but also experiencing the redeemed speech of Pentecost, so too have Americans read their own history as a movement toward or away from the dream of a common tongue and the nightmare of an old Babel, and the narrative of *American Pastoral* recapitulates in microcosm this drama of language that we can find deep within the American story. Confronted by the dissonance of voices in the Constitutional Convention during the drafting of Constitution, Benjamin Franklin feared that without the "concurring aid" of God the committee members "shall succeed in this political building no better, than the builders of Babel: We shall be divided by our local interests; our projects will be confounded, and we ourselves shall become a reproach and bye word down to the future ages."[2] But at the end of the convention, Franklin expresses his faith that the creation of the Constitution "will astonish our enemies, who are waiting to hear with confidence that our councils are confounded like those of the builders of Babel."[3] Ralph Waldo Emerson sees, feels, and hears the coming of this Pentecostal moment in the act of conversation: "Yet let us enjoy the cloven flame whilst it grows on our walls," he comments in his essay

"Circles."[4] The Pentecostal moment he is referring to encompasses not the nation at large but merely the participants in a conversation, and the moment is as short-lived as communion between Jim Dwyer and Lou Levov at the Thanksgiving dinners at the Levovs, but no less significant as a sign of Babel yielding to a higher consensus: "The parties are not to be judged by the spirit they partake and even express under this Pentecost. To-morrow they will have receded from this high-water mark."[5] Emerson champions the moment when "each new speaker strikes a new light, emancipates us from the oppression of the last speaker to oppress with the greatness and exclusiveness of his own thought, then yields us to another redeemer."[6] At the end of *The Crying of Lot 49*, set in the same era as Roth's *American Pastoral*, Thomas Pynchon leaves Oedipa Maas awaiting the crying of "Lot 49," the Pentecostal moment that will gift her with the grace to bring Pierce Inverarity's will into "pulsing, stelliferous meaning," but he leaves readers, as Oedipa herself is left, confronting a world that has "lost the direct, epileptic Word, the cry that might abolish the night": it is a world of competing and confusing and discordant and unheard or muted voices as much as the dinner conversation that concludes *American Pastoral*.[7] In both novels, no moment of unity, no harmony, no transcendence of discord, no e pluribus unum, emerges from the clash of debate and conversation, and instead Roth leaves us remembering the highwater mark of the Pentecostal moment at the Thanksgiving table of the Levovs in Old Rimrock when Jim Dwyer, before his death in 1959, and Lou Levov commune about the past of Newark and Elizabeth.

The city in America culture has always been the locus of Babel, while the suburb or the small town has been the locus of linguistic harmony (however much subverted in works of the American fiction of the small town). Roth's *American Pastoral*, however, gives us the bucolic small town as the place of discord, whether it be Swede Levov and Bill Orcutt on the field of a pickup football game or the increasingly irreconcilable differences within the Levov family itself. Not just the perspectives on the history of Morris County through the voices of Bill Orcutt and Bucky Robinson are different, but so too are the voices of Swede and his daughter Merry, and Swede and his brother Jerry, and Swede and his father Lou. "The curse of Babel," W. H. Auden suggests, "is not the fact there are many diverse languages—diversity in itself is a good—but the idolization by each linguistic group of its own tongue."[8] Old Rimrock, Swede first imagines, is the place where there can be an overcoming of the idolization of any one tongue, any one religion. But the world of Old Rimrock in the 1960s is America writ small: it is a town, a suburb, a city, a country as torn apart by the idolization of separate tongues for Swede (and Roth) as antebellum America was for Hawthorne and Melville and so many other writers in that age of civil and uncivil conflict. In 1848, James Russell Lowell, as part of his condemnation of the actions and orations of Manifest Destiny that led to the Mexican–American War, gives voice to Homer Wilbur, A.M., the purported editor of *The Biglow Papers*, who offers an annotation on the Babel story: By "speech-making," Wilbur observes, we make ourselves "unintelligible, to our fellows," and he claims "Babel was the first Congress, the earliest mill erected for the manufacture of gabble."[9] Just as Lowell and Melville and Whitman and Hawthorne and Emerson each in their own way give us profound meditations on an antebellum America split apart in a babel of tongues and in need of a Pentecostal spirit, so too can we see Roth giving us in his representation of the late 1960s in *American Pastoral* an America as frazzled in dissonance as the Southern California of Pynchon's *Crying of Lot 49* and the Washington, D.C. of Norman Mailer's *Armies of the Night* and Roth's own *Our Gang*, with each of these texts having as its subtext, as much as does Lowell's *Biglow Papers* and Melville's *Moby-Dick*, a war of empire.

Amid the pre–Civil War of tongues and monomaniacal oratory that is antebellum America, Melville gives us the communion of Ishmael and Queequeg, a bonding that occurs when a brother is seen in the other such as happens between Natty Bumppo and Chingachgook in the Leatherstocking novels of James Fenimore Cooper and between Huck and Jim on the raft in Mark Twain's *Adventures of Huckleberry Finn*. Similarly, Roth gives us in *American Pastoral* in a time before the 1960s the communion of Jim Dwyer and Lou Levov and the communion in marriage of Seymour Swede Levov and Mary Dawn Dwyer themselves. But the harmony at the Thanksgiving table in that pre-1960s era between the Levovs and Dwyers, which is initially made possible by the contractual negotiation between Lou Levov and Dawn Dwyer that reconciles the religious differences between the Jewish Levovs and the Catholic Dwyers, becomes, in the era of Watergate, Nixon, and the film *Deep Throat*, at the Levov's dinner party a table of otherhood stained by blood drawn.

When the Levovs convene a congress of voices for the dinner party they host at their home in Old Rimrock in the "Paradise Lost" section, Jesse Orcutt drinks too much. She ends up stabbing Lou Levov in the eye with a fork while he is feeding her rhubarb-strawberry pie and trying to help her sober up. Marcia Unmanoff laughs in mockery at the "pillars of a society"—Bill and Seymour et al.—falling down (p. 423). It is not the fall of Rome, but the fall of Old Rimrock as an Arcadia. Seymour remains immune to the criticism of this professor of English, averring in conclusion, "And what is wrong with their life? What on earth is less reprehensible than the life of the Levovs?" (p. 423). We never get Marcia's answer to this question from Seymour, but, as Roth knows, there would be a gaggle of English professors responding to this question, as there should be, and he has a last word against them in the novel, making a caricature of a feminist English professor in the person of Marcia, just as he makes a caricature of a New Left Vietnam protestor in the figure of Merry.

Roth's *American Pastoral*—and his canon of novels, like those of Thomas Pynchon and John Updike—offer us a way to chart the course of America in the post–World War II era. These works of literature are peopled with types from the regions and times they explore, be it 1960s California by Thomas Pynchon in *The Crying of Lot 49*, *Vineland*, and *Inherent Vice* or 1950s–60s New Jersey in *Goodbye, Columbus* and *American Pastoral*. Just as Roth's Newark could use the voice of an Amiri Baraka and Curtis Lucas (author of the novel *Newark Third Ward*) as a complement and counterpoint to represent Newark through a literary (and biographical) perspective, any study of the Garden State of myth and literature needs to complement the canon of Roth's work with the visions and voices of Junot Díaz and Rick Moody and *Harold and Kumar Go to White Castle* and *The Station Agent* and Kevin Smith's movies (including *Dogma*) and those by Todd Solondz particularly *Happiness* and Nick Gomez's *New Jersey Drive* combined with the music of Bruce Springsteen and the

Fugees and Bon Jovi and Franki Valli (born Francesco
Castelluccio in Newark) and Cissy and Whitney Houston
and Sarah Vaughan and Gloria Gaynor (all four from
Newark too) and Frank Sinatra (born in Hoboken) and
add to that *The Sopranos* and the Stephanie Plum myster-
ies of Janet Evanovich (set in Trenton) and the poetry of
Robert Pinsky (from Long Branch where Norman Mailer
spent some summers) and Christopher Merrill and Steven
Cramer from Brookside and John McPhee on *The Pine
Barrens* and perhaps Paul Auster (born in Newark and
raised in South Orange) and put them all around a dinner table with Dorothy Parker (who attended finishing
school at Miss Dana's School for Young Ladies in Morristown) discussing New Jersey, its literature and history
and culture, with topics for conversation including the literature of Stephen Crane from Newark, New Jersey, buried in Hillside, and William Carlos Williams and Allen
Ginsberg and Judith Ortiz Cofer from Paterson or Walt
Whitman (who lived in Camden from 1873 to his death
in 1892), and add to this conversation the voice of the
anthropologist Sherry Ortner whose study, *New Jersey
Dreaming: Capital, Culture, and the Class of 1958*, traces
the lives of everyone who graduated in 1958 from Weequahic High School in Newark, with Philip Roth its most
famous alumnus, and we can see the dinner table conversation resembling not the poking in the eye with a fork but
the communion of Lou Levov and Jim Dwyer.[10]

17. The Community Club and Its Dissidents

When Philip Roth in *American Pastoral* describes Old
Rimrock, based on Brookside, as basically "one street," he

comments on the Community Club (p. 167). It occupies one of the four corners of the center of Brookside, facing the baseball field with the post office on the opposite corner and the municipal building across the street. The Community Club building was originally the school located where the municipal building is now. It was moved to its current location when a larger school was built to replace the old one. It is supported by annual dues by its members ($50 per year is the minimum). Membership is open to all who live in Mendham Township, so it is not exclusive. Its members host the Fourth of July parade as well as an Easter egg hunt, a clam bake, and a holiday bazaar. It is used too for meetings of the Boy Scouts and Girl Scouts, art and yoga classes, and it can be rented for birthdays, weddings, and large family gatherings. It retains, even if more in symbolism than fact, an essential part of Brookside identity. "Our little club has served as a gathering place for our town in the best of times and in the worst of times."[1]

In the late 1950s, Brookside experienced a sequence of arsons. An arsonist set fire to Bockoven's dairy farm on West Main Street, located less than a half mile from the center of town and close to the entrance to Mendham Township's K–8 elementary school. Even more of a conflagration in terms of size and locale was a fire set by the arsonist that burned down the Community Club in 1959 and lit up the night sky over the town center, casting images of this fire through the bedroom windows on the second floor of our home. The fires were probably done by a rebel without a cause. I believe the son of a worker at Bockoven's dairy farm was charged with them. I can only speculate about the arsonist's motivation. But I feel Merry Levov would understand it better than Swede or Bill Orcutt. Did the arsonist possess an anger at the Brookside community not dissimilar from Merry's at the pretenses and stratifications of Old Rimrock? More important, how much did dissent against the Old Rimrock community itself and not just against the Vietnam War figure in Merry's motivations for targeting the post office with a bomb as represented in the novel? How does Swede himself become a figure of such dissent beyond knocking Orcutt on his ass?

Just like Hester Prynne and her act of adultery in *The Scarlet Letter*, Merry and her bombing of the post office are subject to a range of interpretations in *American Pastoral*, with some of the harshest judgments coming not just from voices within the Levov family and from Nathan Zuckerman but also from an assemblage of voices from the Old Rimrock community and her Morristown high school. These judgments are sounded in the voices of the weekly newspapers local to the area and from a range of newspapers in the outer metropolitan areas including "the New York papers—the *Times*, the *Daily News*, the *Daily Mirror*, the *Post*; in the Jersey dailies—the *Newark News*, the *Newark Star-Ledger*, the *Morristown Record*, the *Bergen Record*, the *Trenton Times*, the *Paterson News*; in the nearby Pennsylvania papers—the *Philadelphia Inquirer*, the *Philadelphia Bulletin*, and the *Easton Express*; and in *Time* and *Newsweek*" (p. 170). The narrative of *American Pastoral* also riffs on Merry's bombing in relation to a lineup of New Jersey crimes such as the Lindbergh kidnapping and on the "region's slender history of atrocities," including when the narrative names Brookside for its only time when it references a murder in Brookside by "an inmate who had walked off the grounds of the Greystone mental asylum, visited his uncle in Brookside, and split the man's head open with an ax" (p. 170). Roth's novel in effect updates post–Puritan era scandalmongering at the local community level. The *Newark News* and *Morristown Record* "in particular would not let up . . . churning out their stories about the Rimrock Bomber every single day for weeks" (p. 170). Inside the Community Club with its talk during its "chicken suppers" and voting, there are "varying degrees of sympathy or of contempt" expressed (p. 168). Swede also "receives anti-Semitic mail" and "overhears things," as does Dawn: "What can you expect? They have no business being out here to begin with" (p. 168). "An editorial from the local paper, recording the tragedy and commemorating Dr. Conlon, is thumbtacked to the Community Club bulletin board and hangs there, right out by the street" (p. 168). It "not only remains intact but is almost completely legible for one whole year" (p. 168). The reverend from the First Congregational Church (the denomination of the church in Brookside on East Main Street) in his sermon on the bombing "sought to find some good in all the tragedy" and "Rev. James Viering of St. Patrick's Church" (there is a St. Joseph's Catholic church in Mendham Borough) gives "an impassioned homily" on it (p. 169). Another clipping posted on the Community Club board gives a report of an interview with Edgar Bartley, a high school classmate of Merry's who had taken her on a date to the movies in Morristown, in which he is quoted: "I never thought she would do something like this. . . . I knew her as a very nice girl. I never heard her say anything vicious. I'm sure something snapped" (p. 169).

Among this pillory of reporting and gossip and alongside the preaching and offhand speculation, what most disturbs Swede is a local newspaper's article that appears to give the fullest reporting on Merry from those who knew her outside of her family circle. The article is entitled,

"SUSPECTED BOMBER IS DESCRIBED AS BRIGHT, GIFTED BUT WITH 'STUBBORN STREAK'" (p. 171). For Swede, it is as if this article puts Merry in public stocks. It is not posted on the Community Club bulletin board, but Swede imagines that if it was, he would have to tear it down. The article begins with rather innocuous comments about Merry and much nicer ones about her than we ever get from Zuckerman and Jerry Levov: she "was known as a multi-talented child, an excellent student and somebody who never challenged authority. People looking to her childhood for some clue about her alleged violent act remained stymied when they remembered her as a cooperative girl full of energy" (p. 171). The article cites remarks by the principal of Old Rimrock Community School: "We are in disbelief. It is hard to understand why this happened" (p. 171). As a student, she was "very helpful and never in trouble. She's not the kind of person who would do that. At least not when we knew her here" (p. 171). The article also describes the principal calling her "a straight A" student who was "well liked by both students and faculty," and the principal gives Merry more praise, noting that she was a "talented art student and a leader in team sports, particularly kickball," and the quoted remarks of the principal conclude "She was just a normal kid growing up" (pp. 171–172). The article then cites remarks from her classmates at Morristown High School who remember "the alleged bomber's stubborn streak" and that she was "arrogant and superior to everybody else" (p. 172). They also remember her "lashing out in anger" if somebody opposed her "thinking about the presence of American troops in Vietnam," while her homeroom teacher in high school remembers her "working hard and doing well," with an "interest in attending . . .

Penn State" (p. 172). What upsets Swede the most about
the article is its headline about her "stubborn streak."
Indeed, nothing written about Merry and her bombing
wounds Swede "as savagely" as this highlighting of her
"stubborn streak" (p. 171). Swede responds to it according
to Zuckerman with his own most pointed critique against
Old Rimrock: "There is something concealed there—yet
implicit—a degree of provincial smugness, of simplemind-
edness, of sheer stupidity that is so enraging to him"
(p. 171). Swede's vehement reaction to this article demands
a review of Merry's own opinions that listens more care-
fully to dissent against Old Rimrock sounded in the novel
as in this instance here by Swede and especially Merry's
own words. This dissent against Old Rimrock is too
smothered in the novel by Swede's own embrace of the
place as the fulfillment of a dream and by the vehemence
of Jerry's and Nathan's damnation of Merry.

We know why Swede chooses to move to Old Rimrock
and embrace all that is symbolized by its Community
Club as well as the treasure of his magnificent old stone
house and its one hundred acres. But what motivates Merry's dissidence? Why did Merry bomb the post office?
"What *is* the grudge? What *is* the grievance? That was the
central mystery: how did Merry get to be who she is?"
(p. 138). These questions asked by Nathan Zuckerman
become the questions that animate so much of the novel,
turning its narrative into a debate, often angry, with each
answer a revelation as much about the character who gives
it as it is about Merry. The questions are asked in different ways time and again in the novel, and the answers
range from the psychological to the political and social
and international including the horrors of the American
war in Vietnam as a trauma for Merry. Some among the

community of scholars of this novel have themselves
tended in part to gang up on Merry following the lead of
the two characters who dominate the novel in answer-
ing these questions and characterizing Merry: Nathan
Zuckerman, as the narrator of the story, and Jerry Levov,
as his key informant about Merry as well as Swede's life in
Old Rimrock. Like the articles posted on the Community Club bulletin board and from the local weekly that is
not posted on that board, Nathan's voice is the communal one. Among scholars, Pia Masiero has best taught
readers how to read Nathan's voice not as a narrative
mirror but as a lamp that shines light on voices from its
own angle of vision.[2] Nathan's voice orchestrates the
other voices, and it gives fortissimo to Jerry's. Nathan
depends primarily on Jerry and his judgments.

Jerry Levov's voice is the most caustic in the novel, and
he eviscerates Merry: "She was miserable, self-righteous—
little shit was no good from the time she was born"
(p. 69). "She did not belong to anything that you were"
(p. 71). "She was out of bounds, a freak of nature, *way* out
of bounds" (p. 71). "The angry kid who gets nuttier and
nuttier" (p. 71). "The little shit, the selfish little fucking
shit, playing her fucking games with you!" (p. 281). Jerry
does scattershot blaming. She is paying "everybody back
for her stuttering" (p. 73). She hates her father. He also
turns his visceral dissent not just at Swede and his wife but
directly at the world of Old Rimrock: "Out there with
Miss America, dumbing down and dulling out. Out there
playing at being Wasps" (p. 280). "*I* would have thrown a
bomb . . . That Wasp bullshit!" (p. 280).

Nathan echoes and lights up Jerry's thunder and light-
ning at Merry—"the monster daughter" (p. 67), "the

hater—this insurrectionist child!" (p. 138), "Ignorant little fucking bitch!" (p. 214), "angry, idiot child" (p. 226). He does his own scattergun blaming, making her politics the personal and the psychological: "It seemed that the etiology of Merry's problem had largely to do with her having such good-looking and successful parents" (pp. 95–96). "What was the whole sick enterprise other than angry, infantile egoism thinly disguised as identification with the oppressed?" (p. 134). For Nathan, it has "nothing whatsoever to do with 'ideals' but with dishonesty, criminality, megalomania, and insanity. Blind antagonism and an infantile desire to menace" (p. 206). Or for Nathan: "All of it because the mother was once Miss New Jersey?" factored in with "rebellious adolescence" and Merry's own ugliness (p. 243). For a moment, Nathan does pick up Swede's wondering and hints at the problem of the "Rimrock expectations" of her "parents and teachers and friends" (p. 101). But unlike Jerry and more like Swede, Nathan appears too enamored of Old Rimrock's setting in nature to feel the social dissent of Merry at this nuclear community of Old Rimrock. For Nathan the pastoral is the antidote to the political. He goes Emersonian and Thoreauvian, reflecting on this natural world and a younger Merry embracing it: "here in the lovely Morris County countryside that had been tamed over centuries by ten American generations, back walking the hilly roads that were edged" with "all the flowers she had learned to identify and classify as a 4-H Club project" and then taught her father, "a city boy, to recognize" (p. 419). "In the woods too," Emerson writes, "a man casts of his years, as the snake his slough, and at what period soever of life, is always a child. . . . In the woods, we return to reason and faith. There I feel nothing can befall me in life,—no disgrace, no calamity . . . which nature cannot repair."[3]

The narrative as it nears its end returns us to Merry as a child in the nature of this place: "Indian Brook flowing rapidly on her left, crossed by little bridges, dammed up for swimming holes along the way and opening into the strong trout stream where she'd fished with her father—Indian Brook crossing under the road, flowing eastward from the mountain where it arises" (p. 420). It is stunning how Roth captures the feel of this place and its botany. This Newark-born writer goes deep American romantic in these woods. Roth adds from the perspective of his own innocence: this is a "landscape that for so long now has been bound up with the idea of solace, of beauty and sweetness and pleasure and peace" (pp. 420–421). The irony is what is hidden in this nature. Brookside has its origins as a little Newark, a small Paterson: a place of mills—grist mills, sawmills, tanneries, powered by its streams with falls. And the irony—that Merry knows—is its social world is not distant from a Newark in its own stratifications, and it is her anger at this community that makes that darkness hidden in the green world visible.

Jerry tells his brother Swede: "You wanted Miss America? Well, you've got her, with a vengeance—she's your daughter! You wanted to be a real America jock, a real American marine, a real American hotshot with a beautiful Gentile babe on your arm? You longed to belong like everybody else to the United States of America? Well, you do now, big boy, thanks to your daughter. The reality of this place is right up in your kisser now. With the help of your daughter you're as deep in the shit as a man can get, the real American crazy shit. America amok! America amuck!" (p. 277). "No," Jerry adds, "you didn't make the war. You made the angriest kid in America. Ever since she was a kid, every word she *spoke* was a bomb" (p. 279). Jerry believes he knows the inside story of Merry and also Old Rimrock better than Seymour (and knows Seymour better than Seymour knows himself).

Swede, trying to understand his daughter, recognizes that she has "gone over the edge of the ship" and that he must rescue her (p. 244). He wonders how and why she went overboard, even speculating about the effect of a kiss he gave her when she was eleven and perhaps too from following a new religion that set her over and against his own religion, which is—maybe too unfairly—the religion of the "profit principle" and seeing Old Rimrock as "paradise" (pp. 260, 262). "Tell me where you studied religions," he asks Merry. "In libraries," she answers. "Nobody looks for you there. I was in libraries often, and so I read. I read a lot" (p. 244). A small public library—the Mendham Township Library—was housed in the 1960s on the ground floor of the municipal building, kitty-corner to the post office in Brookside, and it was a place where readers could find voices (as I did and maybe Merry did too) from far outside of Brookside, possibly taking young readers like Merry into the trials and troubles of injustice and racism around the world and closer to home as well. As a young kid, she would swing on trees in their backyard that were for Swede "precious moments" that "symbolized" "the realization of his every hope," but Merry "worried about" and "loved Algeria" (p. 326). Roth gives us his reading list of books that shaped him coming of age and later, which includes near the top Howard Fast's *Citizen Tom Paine*. I wish we could look at Merry's library card for what she checked out and learned from that helped her see Old Rimrock and America from a different point of view than Swede's.[4]

Merry Levov bombs the Old Rimrock post office at the age of sixteen. Middle-class and upper-middle-class student protest against the Vietnam War in the community of teens in a place like Old Rimrock or Brookside is better represented to me by dissident high school students carrying a coffin at the end of the Fourth of July parade and sitting down in front of the Community Club during the playing of the national anthem from its steps than Merry Levov's bombing of the post office. "You can be against the war at the Community Club," Swede advises Merry (p. 112). Merry scoffs at her dad's suggestion: "All twenty people" (p. 112). But a set of students Merry's age did do this, and at least one of the same group of students from Brookside in the Fourth of July protest had earlier participated in an all-night vigil against the Vietnam War on the Green in Morristown's center at the end of June. Merry herself had first turned her "living room" at home into a "battlefield," then Morristown High (p. 113). It is such protests—and students marching nonviolently in moratoriums and celebrating at Woodstock and buying the records of Bob Dylan and Jimi Hendrix that seemed like noise to parents who loved Frank Sinatra as well as watching a new generation of movies that featured rebels with a cause beginning with *The Graduate*—that helped tumble a few fence posts of the walled gardens of suburban America, be it in Beverly Hills or Brookside. Mark Shechner makes an apt comment when he notes in his chapter on *American Pastoral* in *Up Society's Ass* that "Roth missed the musical boat" by not giving to Merry "a soundtrack of her own as a radical during a decade that was galvanized by music."[5] Here would be "the backbeat to Merry's turbulence" that would bring "some credibility" to Merry "as a creature of her time, not simply as a symptom of suburban anomie."[6] Merry is a creature of her turbulent time, but her dissent is belittled for me by calling it a "symptom of suburban anomie." Her dissent is a mix in large part of fury and fire and disturbance against LBJ's prosecution of the Vietnam War—and from her first traumatic experience of that war at the age of ten or eleven seeing on television "the self-immolation of the Buddhist monks"—but it also is dissent against Swede's vision of Old Rimrock as a falsification of her own experience of the place and as a betrayal rather than fulfillment of America ideals (p. 152). "What the Swede never understands," as Sandra Kumamoto Stanley argues so well in one of the best essays on *American Pastoral*, is "how his pastoral vision of America could give birth to Merry's anger."[7] Merry's anger rises against not just American imperialism and militarism and capitalism but also Swede's pastoral vision of Old Rimrock in contrast to how she sees and experiences Old Rimrock and its community of people: "They just want to go to b-bed at night, in their own country, leading their own lives, and without thinking they are going to get b-b-blown to b-b-b-b-b-bits in their sleep. B-b-blown to b-b-b-b-bits all for the sake of the privileged people of New Jersey leading their p-p-peaceful, s-s-secure, acquisitive, meaningless l-l-l-little bloodsucking lives!" (p. 108). Here is the local habitation of "immorality" of the "bourgeois life" that Merry first "was blasting away at the dinner table" (p. 240). She claims "that there never could be a revolution in America to uproot the forces of racism and reaction and greed," and Merry knows these roots so well because she has bitten into the apple of Old Rimrock while her dad has been out there playing "Johnny Apple-seed" (p. 260). Merry, in effect, does to Old Rimrock what rioters did to Newark in 1967, and the etiology of each explosion is not entirely dissimilar.

The local weekly newspaper for the Mendhams, the *Observer-Tribune*, carried a report on the antiwar protest at the Brookside Fourth of July parade in 1969 led by Ken Lurie and Steven Cramer in its July 10th issue that can offer us not just more reason to appreciate Roth's gifts of intuition and his felt sense of history in *American Pastoral* but also a deeply resonant perspective on Merry's act of dissent in her bombing of the Old Rimrock Post Office and general store as symbolic. Entitled, "Peaceful War Protest Ends Brookside Parade," the article describes in its opening how "a group of township youths, marching at the end of the parade. . . . quietly protested United States involvement in the Vietnam War" by carrying a "mock coffin" and "passing out leaflets to parade watchers."[8] It notes that one of the female protestors "wore a long black robe and had her face painted to resemble a skull" and carried "a poster with the words, 'Stop the War in Vietnam Now' and a picture reminiscent in part of Pablo Picasso's masterpiece of anti-war painting, 'Guernica.'" The article explains the protestors were part of a group that called itself "Members of the New Community of Morris County" and that they passed out a leaflet entitled "The Dead Enemy," which said in part, "America's enemy is not communism, is not poverty, is not demonstrations," but is the "dead enemy, that citizen who ignores his responsibilities and duties which are required of those who live in a democracy." The leaflet adds, "A democracy is form of government in which each individual maintains a knowledgeable, informed opinion even when it is opposition to popular sentiment. When a citizen fails to participate in democracy, that form of government falters. That individual is a 'dead enemy.'" The group also passed out leaflets that asked if people had "informed opinions on the 1964 Geneva Accords" and if they knew the names of the president and vice president of South Vietnam and distributed a "Questions and Answers on Vietnam pamphlet." At the end of the parade, on the grounds of the baseball field facing the Community Club, the protestors "stood the casket up on end and revealed a mirror attached to it with the words, 'the dead enemy' over them." The article indicates that "several residents became angry at the group when they remained sitting during the Pledge of Allegiance to the flag." It adds that an "informal complaint was made to the parade committee" and that a "few harsh words were directed at the protestors" and that after a committee member informed the protestors of a complaint and at "the suggestion of the police and parade organizers," they "left the area."

Merry's dissent against the Vietnam War—and against the "dead enemy" of the residents of Old Rimrock—begins at the decibel level of this rhetoric and then it escalates in her home before it becomes the bomb. But it never seems to be part of a chorus among her classmates at Morristown High or among civic activists in Morristown her age such as can be found among "Members of the New Community of Morris County." When Merry explodes her dissent, becoming the "Rimrock Bomber," she directs her attack at the office of letters, almost in the shadow of George Washington's Headquarters in Morristown, an act that the newspaper articles posted on the Community Club bulletin board fathom less than the one posted in *The Observer-Tribune* about the July 4, 1969, parade protest.

What one of the protestors at the Brookside Fourth of July parade communicated to me in an email message as the "hellishness" of growing up in Brookside is a more imploded sound, but Roth helps us hear that too in *American Pastoral* through the voice and actions of Merry before the bombing.

Brookside, for me, coming of age so close to the center of town with its library, a baseball field, and my elementary school and with woods and a stream on one side of our home and a horse in our barn and a corral in an upper lot, was at once a civic community, a pastoral playground, and a frontier town. But it would become for me, perhaps strange to understand for many a child who came of age in the same era in Newark, a place I desperately wanted to leave for a city, just as Merry wants to leave Old Rimrock for New York City, and I knew that if I looked homeward, as I am doing now, it would be more as a fallen angel, a Lucifer who would return to this "garden place" not just with very dear memories of how fortunate I felt to grow up here but also with a desire to hurl verbal bombs at Brookside, exploding its conceits, exposing its secrets and scandals: a tax collector cooking the tax books and then burning them, our police chief torching a hippie hangout, successful NIMBYism to block a county jail site in Morris Township, enough affairs to delight John Updike, my Sunday school teacher in a wife-swapping circle, WASP kids in the school on the last day before winter vacation wishing others "Happy Hanukkah" as an insult, insidious anti-Black racism, a mother of four kids killed in an alcohol-induced car crash on Route 24 between Mendham and Brookside on the way back from a night of drinking with her husband, an alumnus from Yale and a neighbor ranting about the school accepting too many minorities, my father calling Black kids playing in the streets of Morristown unprintable names as we drove through the town, corporate executives on the planning board and in town overlooking a zoning violation or making an exception for the pro shop at their private golf course, and the overall relative invisibility of the walls that made my home a place of prejudice and exclusion, not a world elsewhere, not a world immune from history, not a world of escape, not a place of freedom from injustice, but a place impinged on by history and shaped by a politics that made it as un-Arcadian and as stained with the human as Roth's Newark.

18. *American Pastoral* and Revolutions of the Word

What Philip Roth reminds us of in *American Pastoral*— and what the American Revolution should remind us of too, as does so much of American literature, indeed this is one of its great themes—is that we can reinvent ourselves not through changing a place, moving from here to there, but through a change of words. The transformation is through language and logos, the word and the book. We change ourselves, we transform ourselves, we revolutionize ourselves by changing the story, telling a new story, reading a different story, listening to a different story, learning a new language, escaping Eden and embracing Babel. Every revolution, Roland Barthes argues, demands a transformation of the established language.[1] The American Revolution was first and foremost a linguistic action, and its primary actions in the preface to the Declaration of Independence in July 1776 involved the teaching and learning of a new language and the criticism of an old language, a revolt against the king and Parliament begun not with a tea party and a battle on Lexington Green and Concord Bridge, but begun with salvos of speeches and sermons by Jonathan Mayhew and Sam Adams and a pamphlet by Thomas Paine: a rebellion that was a revolt against the King's English, a combat against linguistic as well as a political misrepresentation, a war of the rap voice of a Patrick Henry and the prophetic and punk voice of a Tom Paine and the country western voice of sincerity of a Thomas Jefferson converging in slang-whanging that "sticks it to the man." The Revolution began, in language that borrows from Langston Hughes's poem "In Explanation of Our Times," when the folks with no titles in front of their names talked back to the folks called mister, which remains the fundamental process of change and transformation in American politics and culture (be that change progressive or reactionary). This is how Oliver Wendell Holmes describes this transformation in *The Professor at the Breakfast Table*:

> Language! The blood of the soul, Sir! into which our thoughts run and out of which they grow! We know what a word is worth here in Boston. Young Sam Adams got up on the stage at Commencement out at Cambridge there, with his gown on, the Governor and Council looking on in the name of the Majesty, King George the Second, and the girls looking down out of the galleries, and taught people how to spell a word that wasn't in the Colonial dictionaries! *R-e, re, s-i-s, sis, t-a-n-c-e, Resistance.* That was in '43, and it was a good many years before the Boston boys began spelling it with their muskets;—but when they did

begin, they spelt it so loud that the old bedridden women in the English almshouses heard every syllable! Yes, yes, yes,—it was a good many years before those other two Boston boys got the class so far along that it could spell those two hard words, *Independence* and *Union*! I tell you what, Sir, there are a thousand lives, aye, sometimes a million, go to get a new word into a language that is worth speaking. We know what language means too well here in Boston to play tricks with it. We never make a new word till we have made a new thing or a new thought, Sir! When we shaped the mould of this continent, we had to make a few. When, by God's permission, we abrogated the primal curse of maternity, we had to make a word or two. The cutwater of this great Leviathan clipper, the OCCIDENTAL,—this thirty-masted wind-and-steam wave-crusher,—must throw a little spray over the human vocabulary as it splits the waters of a new world's destiny![2]

Merry Levov has a stutter. She is not fluent in the language of protest. She never smooths out her stuttering "R-e, re, s-i-s, sis, t-a-n-c-e, tance" into "Resistance," a voice that gets heard, a voice that performs an action. Her political frustration becomes a frustration with the power of language and letters, the means that her grandfather uses incessantly to voice his protests. Merry turns to a bomb. The colonists, frustrated with an England that did not listen and respond to their petitions, their representations, responded with the shot heard round the world and the bomb of a war led by George Washington, whose home for two winters during the Revolution is in the same town where Merry goes to school, the same town where one can find not just

George Washington's Headquarters but a statue of Thomas Paine, with a musket across his lap as he pens the first of his *The Crisis* essays with his quill as his sword: "These are the times that try men's souls."[3]

In America, in the word, we trust. The United States is, as Washington Irving terms it, a logocracy, a place where we do battle through the word, through slang-whanging and speechifying, through oratory and letter writing, through op-ed pieces and debate, blah, blah, blah. Democracy is the place where the battlefield of the sword and arms is replaced by the battlefield of the forum: the word against the word. Or so we hope. But in America: In gun, we trust. The Morristown of Merry, of *American Pastoral*, is the Morristown of George Washington's sword, not Thomas Paine's word. The America of the Cold War, the America of the Civil War, the America of the war against American Indians, against Mexico, against Spain, against Japan, against Germany, against communism, against Saddam Hussein, against terrorism, is the America of "In Gun We Trust."

But the American Revolution of Philip Roth and the American Civil War of Philip Roth, as he revealed to us in the second novel of his American Trilogy, *I Married a Communist*, is the America of Thomas Paine and Abraham Lincoln, of battle and victory through the word as much as the sword, transforming the rage of Achilles into the ire of Ira Ringold, who with his brother, Murray, a veteran of World War II who has become a teacher, is transforming the fight against fascism into a battle of words, a battle of facts, a battle of words and facts combined together. The literary method of Roth in his American Trilogy is the literary method of Thomas Jefferson's Declaration of Independence: style and eloquence articulating

facts to do battle against tyranny. This is from the conclusion of Jefferson's first section of the Declaration: "let facts
be submitted to a candid world."[4] This is so much the
method of Roth as a writer, grounding his fiction, his storytelling, meticulously in fact. Jefferson tells a story, and
he supports it with facts that give as he writes near the end
of the Declaration the "last stab to agonizing affection"
(p. 23). Roth engages in his pursuit of happiness and freedom and a more perfect union as a writer by telling stories supported by facts. His storytelling, his style, his
eloquence, is modeled not just after Thomas Jefferson or
John Adams but Paine and Lincoln. The way to defeat
King George III, the way to defeat John Calhoun, the way
to defeat Joseph McCarthy, the way to defeat Tricky Dick,
the way to defeat Trump as a confidence man, is to tell a
better story, grounded in facts, that exposes the tricks of
language of these cons.[5]

Roth's *I Married a Communist* follows *American Pastoral* by a year in order of publication, and although in
terms of chronological times for its setting, it comes before
American Pastoral, set as it is in the 1950s, the McCarthy
era rather than in the era of the Vietnam War and Watergate, we can read it as a sequel to *American Pastoral* if we
read it as a language-teaching lesson on par with how Paine
taught colonists how to fight King George III and how
Lincoln taught people how to fight the tyranny of slavery.
Nathan Zuckerman loves Paine and baseball, and in *I
Married a Communist*, he describes how his "idealism," as
a young man coming of age, "was being constructed along
parallel lines, one fed by novels about baseball champions
who won their games the hard way, suffering adversity and
humiliation and many defeats as they struggled toward
victory, and the other by novels about heroic Americans

who fought against tyranny and injustice, champions of liberty for America and for all mankind" (IMC, p. 25).

Zuckerman becomes fascinated thanks to a novel by Howard Fast with the man whose statue stands out at the entrance to Morristown when driving east from Brookside: the man, Thomas Paine, the novel *Citizen Tom Paine*. "By the time I had finished the book, there seemed to me no way other than Paine's for a man to live and die if he was intent on demanding, in behalf of human freedom—demanding both from remote rulers and from the coarse mob—the transformation of society" (p. 25). "Reading about him," Zuckerman adds, "had made me feel bold and angry and, above all, free to fight for what I believed in" (p. 26). Ira Ringold then becomes Zuckerman's tutor for understanding the significance of Paine. "You know what the genius of Paine was," asks Ringold as a teacher. "To defy the English," a student answers (p. 26). "A lot of people did that," Ringold explains. "No. It was to articulate the cause *in* English. The revolution was totally improvised, totally disorganized. Isn't that the sense you get from this book, Nathan? Well, these guys had to find a language for their revolution. To find the words for a great purpose" (p. 27). Roth creates for Ringold a beautiful, compelling commentary on Paine and the leaders of the Revolution, a commentary that compares to how Oliver Wendell Holmes describes the Revolution as a language-learning lesson in *The Professor at the Breakfast Table*.[6] Ringold and Zuckerman combine here to figure one of Roth's own ideals of himself as a writer and what idealism he has for the power of the word in America. Paine puts aside his musket to use his pen in the symbolism of the statue in Morristown: defiance and protest take the form of verbal action, not violence, hurling a *Common*

Sense or *The Crisis* essays at the British, fighting with the pen not the sword, the letter not the bomb.

Nathan Zuckerman in *I Married a Communist* first comes under the spell of the teaching of Ira Ringold's brother, Murray, who had a special talent, as a teacher, for "dramatizing inquiry," which is Roth's own talent as a writer (IMC, p. 1). Murray also is honored in the opening paragraph of *I Married a Communist* for his commitment to being "strictly analytic and scrutinizing aloud, in his clear-cut way, what we read and wrote" (p. 1). Murray upholds an aesthetic of language as a politics of language, celebrating Abraham Lincoln for writing "as noble and beautiful a sentence as any American president, as any American *writer,* had ever written": the first sentence of the last paragraph of Lincoln's second inaugural address, when Lincoln switches from the Old Testament justice called for in his penultimate paragraph (the eye for an eye of a blood spilt by the lash of the slaveholder repaid with blood spilt by the sword of the Northern army) with the New Testament justice of the first sentence of the concluding paragraph: "With malice toward none, with charity for all. . . . ." (p. 18).

Later in the novel, Nathan Zuckerman comes under the spell of another teacher, Leo Glucksman, a PhD student in literature at the University of Chicago. Zuckerman prefaces his introduction to Glucksman with a meditation of how we can be transformed by the word through the process of choosing "new allegiances and affiliations" from within the home that is the library, finding there "the parents of your adulthood, the chosen parents whom, because you are not asked to acknowledge them with love, you either love or don't, as suits you" (p. 217). Zuckerman calls this new affiliation to authors of the word a "genealogy, that isn't genetic," and explains that these parents are chosen through "a series of accidents and through lots of will" (p. 217). Nathan then names his own genealogy: "I apprenticed myself, from Paine and Fast and Corwin to Murray and Ira and beyond—the men who schooled me" (p. 217). Glucksman himself becomes a significant figure for Zuckerman's apprenticeship as a novelist, giving him instruction in the tenets of faith for a writer in a logocracy, calling on him to believe that the way to fight as an artist in society, the way to use art as a weapon, the way to disarm enemies, the way to rebel against society is "*to write serious literature*" and to "write *well*" (p. 218). "You want a lost cause to fight for?" asks Glucksman rhetorically in his catechism of Nathan, and he then gives the answer that seems to come straight out of Roth's own mouth: "Then fight for the *word*. Not the high-flown word, not the inspiring word, not the pro-this and anti-that word, not the word that advertises to the respectable that you are a wonderful, admirable, compassionate person on the side of the downtrodden and the oppressed. No, for the word that tells the literate few condemned to live in America that you are on the *side* of the word!" (pp. 218–219). Glucksman later adds another article of faith to his logocractic constitution: literature lives in nuance, complication, contradiction, and above all it keeps "the particular alive in a simplifying, generalizing world—that's where the battle is joined" (p. 223). The unstated irony of these complementary imperatives for the writer as articulated by Murray Ringold and Leo Glucksman is that the two apostles of the word that Murray and Ira uphold—Thomas Paine and Abraham Lincoln—deployed their own eloquence to help argue

Americans into supporting the violence of either the American Revolution or the Civil War.

Merry Levov, who becomes almost as tongue-tied before Lyndon Baines Johnson (and before Swede and Dawn) as Billy Budd does before John Claggart, begins as a letter writer, following the example of that passionate letter writer of political protest, her grandfather Lou. "It was during the Vietnam War that Lou Levov began mailing Merry copies of the letters he sent to President Johnson, letters that he had written to influence Merry's behavior more than the president's" (AP, pp. 287–288). The grandfather counsels Merry: "Honey, we live in a democracy. . . . You don't have to go around getting angry with your family. You can write letters" (p. 289). But when her words fail, and after Lou counsels her to make her protests local, she turns to the bomb, planted at the office of letters in Old Rimrock. "If only Merry had fought a war of words, fought the world with words alone. . . . Then Merry's story would not be a story that begins and ends with a bomb but another story entirely. But a bomb. A bomb. A bomb tells the whole fucking story" (pp. 340–341). The log cabins that housed Continental army soldiers for two winter encampments during the Revolutionary War in Jockey Hollow tell a similar story.

When the words of colonial leaders failed, when England seemed "deaf to the voice of justice & consanguinity," the minutemen of Concord fired the shot heard round the world.[7] Murray Ringold loves Lincoln as much as Paine, as does Ringold's brother, Ira, who performs Lincoln on stage in performances at high schools, including Zuckerman's school. Zuckerman comes to love the words of Paine and Lincoln, and so too did Roth. The quest of

Continental army encampment at Jockey Hollow, Morristown
National Historical Park. Bill Coughlin, HMdb.org.

Paine and Lincoln in part was to compose words to transform society; but they were not afraid to call for violence
to transform society either, and they did. Roth's quest is
to illuminate the world through the word, maybe aiding
in the transformation of society in doing so, but never
making that his explicit goal, choosing instead to illuminate us about the power of the word to darken our understanding while also trying to compose beautiful sentences
for great purposes, in particular the purpose of great art:
the creation of sentences that illuminate, that free us, that
unite us, that transport us, and that help us understand
our time and place, our history, in its particulars, including places such as Newark and Old Rimrock and Brookside and Jockey Hollow.

Epilogue

● ● ● ● ● ● ● ● ●

"The Great New Jersey Novel": *American Pastoral* and the Garden State of Letters

Philip Roth's *American Pastoral* is a leading candidate for the great New Jersey novel. What magnifies Roth's achievement in *American Pastoral* is how he recognizes, as do some of the best movies and television shows set in the state (e.g., *The Station Agent* and *The Sopranos*), that in New Jersey the story of us being "frictioned together in a small place" (Susanne Antonetta's phrase from an essay on Elizabeth, New Jersey) is not just the story of the city but the suburb.[1] The suburb is the new place for the old story of America: the immigrant story, the story of exodus, the story of the pursuit of happiness and liberty roadblocked by racism, the story of mixing and merging in the border-lands and of collisions in the crossroads.

Roth's novel is extraordinary in relationship to the literature of New Jersey. If we map the literature of New Jersey by the location of its settings, one could adapt the title of Angus Gillespie and Michael Aaron Rockland's engaging study of the state, *Looking for America on the New Jersey Turnpike*, and just look for this literature in the places that are not far from exits off the New Jersey Turnpike, some a bit west of it but most of it east, especially in northern New Jersey, with Paterson and Newark its hub cities.[2] To fill in the rest of the map one just needs to add some exits off the southern part of the Garden State Parkway for the literature of the Jersey Shore, with Long Branch a hub. Irina Reyn's edited collection of New Jersey memoirs, *Living on the Edge of the World: New Jersey Writers Take on the Garden State*, is telling in this regard: each memoir is identified by a town plus an exit number off the Turnpike or Parkway, leaving places in New Jersey far from any such exit—as Brookside is—beyond the edge, in a no-exit zone.[3]

Ironically, no matter how suburban New Jersey is, and it is very suburban and rural, the literature (and music) about this state that is most compelling is not the literature of its suburbs but the literature and art of its cities and the shore area. Except for Roth's fiction, the best genre for New Jersey literature is the poem or the memoir, and one of the most compelling subjects is that of identity, particularly the twists and turns of ethnic identity in urban spaces such as Newark and Paterson but also in a smaller place such as the Long Branch of Robert Pinsky as he describes it in *Jersey Breaks: Becoming an American Poet*: "to understand my poetry you need to understand our town."[4] And to understand his town, as Pinsky explains it, is to understand a mix and merging of "races and ethnicities, with all the other blends, resistances, suspicions, borrowings, intermarriages, rivalries and molten alloys of American cuisine, art and social life, all concentrated in a seashore resort," a concentration of people in their blendings and resistances and rivalries that is the New Jersey home of Pinsky (and not just Pinsky).[5] Alas, the most banal literature of New Jersey is the literature of the suburb, even though some of it has received critical praise including Rick Moody's *Garden State*, David Gates's *Jernigan*, James Kaplan's *Two Guys from Verona: A Suburban Memoir*, Cathi Hanauer's *My Sister's Bones* and *Sweet Ruin: A Novel*, Tom Perrotta's *Bad Haircut: Stories of the Seventies* and *The Wishbones*, Richard Ford's *Independence Day*, and Frederick Reiken's *The Lost Legends of New Jersey*.

New Jersey has long felt split between its two halves, north and south, culturally, with the Jersey Shore its own shard. It is also a mosaic of 564 municipalities, making it the state with the most municipalities per square mile. These municipalities take pride in each having their own character, so, for example, despite various initiatives and urgings, Mendham Borough and Mendham Township have long had difficulties combining public services, with resistance strong in Mendham Township against closing down its public library in the municipal building in the center of town across from the post office in order to join with Mendham in creating one new public library that serves both towns. The literature of New Jersey itself tends to be local or minimalist or municipality based in its geographic reach. Rare, in my knowledge, is the work of New Jersey literature that transcends one place, one town, one city, one locale, but this is something Roth does in his first novella set in New Jersey—*Goodbye, Columbus*—and this is a practice he returns to in *American Pastoral*, which becomes in Roth's canon a bookend to *Goodbye, Columbus*.[6] Neil Klugman in this story of romantic adventure and border crossing says goodbye at first to the old world of the city of Newark for the new world of suburban Short Hills. But then in the end he says goodbye to that exodus itself as Neil returns, however unwillingly or however broken-heartedly, to Newark and his job at the public library. On the other hand, Swede Levov almost chortles out, with the cry of a rooster, goodbye Newark and hello Old Rimrock. Indeed, one can hear Swede singing the following lines from The Association's "Goodbye, Columbus" (invoked by Roth in *Goodbye, Columbus*) as he imagines himself Johnny Appleseed or as he is driving up the road to his stone house on his return home from his commute to his work at Newark Maid: "Got that look in our eyes / It's a lucky day, just for changin' / Leavin' the old world behind / Lucky day, for walkin' a new road / Just to clear your mind / It's a day for startin' a new way / Tellin' the old one goodbye / Lucky day for gettin' above it / Spread your wings and fly."[7]

American Pastoral is part of Roth's Newark trilogy, his remembering of Newark, but it is also part of his counterlife stories, his stories of suburban escape and crossing over and passing and exodus to a new world. The novel is at once urban and rural: on one side, it is an exit off the New Jersey Turnpike, and on the other side, it is Arcady Hill Road. By telling the story of both these sides of New Jersey, it becomes at once an unusual work of New Jersey literature and a very representative work of American culture: "Why shouldn't I be where I want to be? Why shouldn't I be with *who* I want to be? Isn't that what this country's all about?" Swede says to Dawn (p. 315). "I want to be where I want to be and I don't want to be where I don't want to be. That's what being an American is—isn't it? I'm with you, I'm with the baby, I'm at the factory during the day, the rest of the time I'm out here, and that's everywhere in this world I *ever* want to be. We own a piece of America, Dawn. I couldn't be happier if I tried. I did it, darling, I did it—I did what I set out to do!" (p. 315). Swede exults in "the wonderful new irreproachable existence of husband and father Seymour Levov, Arcady Hill Road, Old Rimrock, New Jersey, USA" (p. 318). Roth adds, "What he had been doing out on the road—which, as though it were a shameful or superficial endeavor, he could not bring himself openly to confess even to Dawn—was making love to his life" (pp. 318–319). Lou Levov protests the cobblestone streets of Newark being torn up by people for the cobblestones. Arcady Hill Road, if perhaps modeled on Stoney Hill Road, which was still a dirt road in 1967 (it was paved soon afterward), is embraced for Swede for its anti-urbanness.

The suburb is the new place for the old story of America: the immigrant story, the pioneer story, the story of exodus, the story of the pursuit of happiness and liberty and a more perfect union and the transformation of the wilderness into cattle range and farm and the rural and then eventually into the suburb. "Increasingly," Lizabeth Cohen writes in *A Consumers' Republic*, her study of the politics of mass consumption in post-war America that focuses so much on the expanding suburban world of northern New Jersey in this era, "people from long-established, often highly industrialized, and, by the end of the war, congested and deteriorating urban centers—whether neighboring New York City or New Jersey's own Newark, Paterson, Passaic, Jersey City, and Elizabeth—left homes near jobs, relatives, and long-established ethnic and religious communities to move to newly built houses farther out, first in Bergen, Essex, Union, Passaic, and Morris Counties, and later in Burlington, Middlesex, Monmouth, and Somerset, much the way Americans of an earlier era had left farms and small towns for beckoning cities."[8] This is what happens in *American Pastoral*, with Swede envisioning himself as a pioneer, as "some frontiersman of old," escaping off into the wilderness of the highlands of Morris County, seeking his greener world, his new Eden, his happiness and that of his wife Dawn, and his daughter, Merry, and leaving behind his established ethnic and religious community represented by Weequahic (p. 310). "In time," Lizabeth Cohen adds, "70 percent of the state's total land area would qualify as suburban, so that by the turn of the twenty-first century New Jersey and Connecticut shared the distinction of being the nation's most suburbanized states."[9]

The New Jersey literature of this suburban world has tended to be the story of white middle-class teenage angst or male midlife crisis. Roth gives us this angst in *American Pastoral*, double time, in the figures of Swede and Dawn and Merry, and also in the figure of Bill Orcutt, just by the way Roth brilliantly describes how and why Orcutt sports his Hawaiian shirts: "According to the Swede's interpretation, all of the guy's [Orcutt's] effervescence seemed rather to go into wearing those shirts—all his flamboyance, his boldness, his defiance, and perhaps, too, his disappointment and his despair" (p. 335). Orcutt becomes the exemplum in this novel of "Wasp blandness" (p. 384), however disguised—or, better yet, revealed—by the flamboyance of his Hawaiian shirts (and probably too by the peacock-colored pants and boldly plaid shorts I can see him wearing at a summer backyard cocktail party or on the golf course that matched the ones many men wore for those occasions in the 1960s). Merry Levov's own teenage angst might have begun in a protest against the world of Hawaiian shirts and peacock slacks and backyard cocktail parties (and it seems to have a close match in the angst of twelve-year-old Dawn Wiener in Todd Solondz's *Welcome to the Doll House*): "Vehemently she renounced the appearance and allegiances of the good little girl who had tried so hard to be adorable and lovable like all the other good little Rimrock girls—renounced her meaningless manners, her petty social concerns, her family's 'bourgeois' values" (p. 101). Then by the time she is into her last years in high school, in 1968, when she is nicknamed by her schoolmates "Ho Chi Levov," this resentment erupts into a vicious critique of the WASP suburban world—the lives of those who "live out here in the privileged middle of nowhere"—that surpasses any critique Rick Moody or David Gates or James Kaplan articulates (pp. 100, 108). What Merry wants to experience—and where she wants to escape to for her freedom and happiness—is New York City: "Haven't you ever heard," she asks her father, "that New York is one of the world's great cultural centers?" (p. 109). "God forbid," she adds, "I should ever get another point of view" (p. 110).

Merry is prone, very prone, to the cliché, and in her rants against Old Rimrock, she unleashes almost every cliché against the suburban world that has made the suburb in the imagination of so many American artists in the American grain such an unholy land.[10] But she is the anti-cliché to the suburban migration story. Countering celebratory stories of the Puritan errand into the wilderness, Andrew Delbanco argues how and why that ordeal can be read as a first chapter in the immigrant story, and he points out the significant number of Puritans who reversed the migration, leaving New England to go back home to old England.[11] Merry, like these Puritans who returned home, and like Neil Klugman initially in *Goodbye, Columbus*, says goodbye to the chosen land of her father, the place at the end of his trail, leaving Old Rimrock as often as she can for New York while in high school, then returning to Newark to live as a Jain, out-Puritanning the Puritans in her asceticism, her renunciation of the material world. Merry's life becomes the counterlife, the counter-pastoral, or an extended cliché of the counterculture (and a prefiguration of the gentrifying hipster) as much as Bill Orcutt— and Swede himself—are figures of the dream, old and new, that settled and suburbanized western Morris County, New Jersey.

"To make our lives matter," Grace Cavalieri writes in an essay entitled "Trenton," "we create cities which are holy." She adds, "We create Trenton as memory. So that we can be awake before we die, we build the city as a place for thanks. Then we invent eternity so we will always have a home."[12] D. J. Waldie in his beautiful book on his Lakewood, California hometown, *Holy Land: A Suburban Memoir*, reminds us similarly how his parents came to regard Lakewood as their own "holy land," with Waldie himself countering the countercultural cliché of American artists in post–World War II America that life in a Lakewood or in a Levittown or in San Fernando Valley of Los Angeles could be no more holy than purgatory as Norman Mailer suggests in one of the more pungent critiques of suburbia in his 1960 essay, "Superman Comes to the Supermarket": "Not all the roots of American life are uprooted, but almost all, and the spirit of the supermarket, that homogeneous extension of stainless surfaces and psycho-analyzed people, packaged commodities, and ranch homes, interchangeable, geographically unrecognizable, that essence of the new postwar SuperAmerica is found nowhere so perfectly as in Los Angeles' ubiquitous acres."[13] For Waldie, however, there is the temptation—if not the need—to make of his hometown of Lakewood what Swede does of Old Rimrock: a holy land, no matter how subur-ban and exclusive and mundane and superficial and racist the place is or was. Such a willful redemption of this pro-fane world is part of the effort that Cavalieri describes by which we make "our lives matter" and give "thanks" to a place because we inevitably must recognize what Roth felt himself so drawn to depict as an artist: "the impact of place on American lives."[14] If our self, our character, our ideology—our soul—is shaped by the impact of our race or our ethnicity and by our social class and gender and sex-ual orientation and by the eras of time through which we have passed in our lives, so too is it shaped by the places we call home.

The American mythology has always been that we can change, reinvent, and re-create ourselves—and pursue lib-erty and happiness and a more perfect union—by chang-ing our place, especially if that change is the one that New England and Virginia and New Jersey first promised and then that the frontier and the West and California prom-ised again and again: an escape from a closed, confined, limiting world to a more open place. But what the paleface pioneer into the West of the nineteenth century discov-ered, in the footsteps of Columbus and John Smith and John Endicott and Daniel Boone and Natty Bumppo, is that when this new Columbus escaped into the wilderness, he did not just confront nature: he ran into other people—particularly people of color, Native Americans first, then later Mexicans and Hawaiians or South Sea islanders (collisions that Herman Melville's novels from *Typee* and *Omoo* to *Mardi*, *Moby-Dick* and *The Confidence-Man* track the best in American literature).

The newest frontier of America—the next contact zone, the new crossroads—is not the borderlands between countries or the crossroads of our cities, but the suburbs, and what the pioneers into suburbs of New Jersey who are marked by differences of ethnicity or religion such as Swede and Harold and Kumar inevitably discover and confront when they journey into the west of northern and southern New Jersey—into territories such as the rolling hills and former farm lands of Morris County—is that this too has been occupied territory: it is the territory that has been owned and guarded by the power and privilege and genteel politeness of the WASP paleface, or the white castle world of Bill Orcutt in *American Pastoral* and of Tom and Daisy Buchanan out in East Egg in *The Great Gatsby*. This has been the estate world of Geraldine Rockefeller Dodge in Madison, New Jersey, and of William P. Bliss in Roxiticus, New Jersey (on the border of Mendham and Bernardsville) and the Pitney estate in the middle of Brookside.[15] This is the green space that would be turned into corporate headquarters in Madison and Morristown and suburban development in Mendham Township and preserved as green in private golf courses (the Roxiticus Country Club and the Mendham Golf & Tennis Club) and county parks and protected Great Swamps or preserved in the campuses of colleges (Drew and Fairleigh Dickinson) and private high schools (Bayley-Ellard and Delbarton). The wealth of Fifth Avenue that transformed this land into estates then gave way to the creation of "groves of academe" and then increasingly to the commercialization and corporatization of these estates, while new money in Mendham Township and surrounding areas helped buy the land—or buy the lobbying of government—to green the way for preserving former private estates as public parks. Corporate executives living in old stone homes in these places—figures such as the Badenhausens of Ballantine and the Mercks of Merck Pharmaceuticals—just like Swede as chief executive of Newark Maid, settled far from their work in this Old Rimrock world of Mendham Township, replicating in a place not too far away the move of one of New Jersey's great industrial pioneers—Thomas Edison—into one of the first planned suburbs in the United States: Llewellyn Park in West Orange.

One by one, through the 1960s and beyond, corporate headquarters and offices moved west to this region too, replacing almost every one of the mansions along Millionaire's Row between Madison and Morristown, New Jersey. Swede Levov moves west out of Newark in the late 1950s. So too did the Mafia boss Richie "The Boot" Boiardo from Newark who built himself a castle home—with a Godfather's Garden—in Livingston (and who became the model for David Chase's Tony Soprano). Newark Academy and Temple B'Nai Abraham would follow the same path in the late 1960s and early 1970s, each moving also from Newark to Livingston, near the home of the Patimkins from *Goodbye, Columbus* in Short Hills. Eventually Chris Christie and Whitney Houston and Joachim Prinz would follow but move further west, fifteen or so miles beyond Livingston, as would the Rabbinical College of America, which moved from Newark to Morris Township in 1971.[16] The convergence of these worlds was once the story of the city told by Henry James, Edith Wharton, and John Dos Passos—and it is the New York City of *The Great Gatsby* too—and escape from this convergence, this mix, with its frictions, is part of the allure of Old Rimrock for Swede. But out in northern west Jersey, this escape becomes the locus for new convergences and new separations and new frictions.

Philip Roth in *American Pastoral* gives us not just the history of Newark and the diaspora of its Jews from the city but a history of Morris County with the same faithful, meticulous attention to detail and fact he is famous for in his writings about the world of Newark in the American Trilogy. This great New Jersey novel, unlike many novels set in New Jersey, has a breadth of geography that crosses beyond the borders of one town, one city, one municipality, giving us states of mind not just from cities of Newark and Elizabeth and the summer resort towns of the Jersey Shore—the New Jersey accessed along the New Jersey Turnpike and the Garden State Parkway—but it also takes us to the original end of the route of the Morris and Essex rail line, one of the first commuter lines in the United States, which began construction in 1835 and completed an extension to Morristown, New Jersey in 1838. Just as the Morris Canal brought coal from the Lehigh Valley in Pennsylvania to the factories of Newark, it was the Morris and Essex rail line that transported white-collar workers from their homes in the Essex and Morris County suburbs—Maplewood, Milburn, Summit, Chatham, Madison, Convent Station, Morristown—to run the factories of finance and insurance of metropolitan New York and New Jersey. It also originally helped bring the high society of Fifth Avenue—the wealth of New York—out to the country, with the rail line between Madison and

Morristown paralleling in its course the stretch of Madison Avenue between Madison and Morristown that became known as Millionaire's Row: an avenue lined with the estates of Daniel Drew (now Drew University), Florence Vanderbilt and Hamilton Twombly (now Fairleigh Dickinson University), Geraldine Rockefeller Dodge (now a complex of corporate headquarters), George Danforth (later Bayley-Ellard Parochial School), and then past Morristown the estate of Luther Kountze (now Delbarton Prep School). To look for America in northern New Jersey, we must look along the rail lines of the old Morris and Essex Railroad, later called the Erie Lackawanna, as much as along the New Jersey Turnpike, as this is the rail line that takes us into the old heart of power and privilege in New Jersey. It takes us as well to the home of the headquarters of George Washington and the encampment of the Continental army in the course of two different winters in the middle of the Revolutionary War.[17]

The history Roth gives us in *American Pastoral* reminds us that there was the violence of the "indigenous American berserk" in Morristown and its surrounding areas long before Merry's bomb exploded, including not just the violence of the Revolution but the explosion in 1926 at Picatinny Arsenal, an American military manufacturing and research facility (located just fourteen miles from Washington's Headquarters in Morristown) that served as a major large-caliber round loading plant with 18,000 employees during World War II and continued to serve as a home for the manufacture of munitions during the Vietnam War when "it gave troops in Vietnam," according to its website, "a complete family of 40mm ammunition for grenade launchers and helicopter gunships."[18] Roth also reminds us of the long history of Jews in Morristown. *The Jews of New Jersey: A Pictorial History*, authored by Patricia M. Ard and Michael Aaron Rockwell, documents in its photos and text part of the history that Bucky Robinson tells Swede as a counterpart to the WASP history tour that Bill Orcutt conducts. It includes photos of Jewish families in Morristown and the Morristown Jewish Center, a temple built in 1929 by Jews who moved from Newark. One of its last chapters, entitled "Anti-Semitism: The Snake in the Garden State," with its haunting picture of a Bund rally of 1,000 marching American Nazis in Andover, New Jersey on July 18, 1937, gives proof as well to Lou Levov's comment: there are haters out there.[19] What is missing from this book, and perhaps what Roth knew from oral history, is the story of the Jewish summer resort community of Mt. Freedom. This absence is analogous in some ways for me to a photo of the Brookside post office missing from the section on Old Rimrock in Hummel's *Journey through Literary America.*

American Pastoral combines in its breadth of geography a willingness to straddle Newark and Old Rimrock, the city and the country, the world of Jew and gentile (and Nazi sympathizers) and inhabit not just the contact zone and borderland worlds of Newark and Elizabeth but that other borderland world where a city has been left behind for the suburb and where the suburb trails off into the rural.[20] The novel combines the horizontal axis of this breadth of geography with a vertical axis of a depth of history, taking us back in history and myth to the Picatinny Arsenal of World War II and the Morristown of George Washington and the Revolution and the Morris and Hunterdon Counties of canals and an iron industry and peach orchards and the Old Rimrock of Johnny

Appleseed, and far beyond that, to Exodus and Genesis, a layering of allusion that makes *American Pastoral* a candidate not just for the Great New Jersey novel, but for one of the great American novels of the second half of the twentieth century.

Just like so many classic American narratives, the ontology of *American Pastoral* recapitulates the philology—the language—of the first two books of the Bible—Genesis and Exodus—and the first two founding documents of the United States: the Declaration of Independence and the Constitution. The genesis of *American Pastoral* is in the Exodus story—the escape from bondage to freedom, the exile from old world to new world—the move of Swede Levov from Newark to Old Rimrock. But like the thematic action of so many classic American narratives, this Exodus story in *American Pastoral* returns us to Genesis and original sins: a loss of innocence, a fall from the garden, betrayal, disobedience. The exodus is never liberation from the past or from the sins of the past. The more the exodus tries to escape the past, the more the past returns to haunt hope for the future with the memory—and nightmares—of history. The United States itself has its genesis in exodus, whether that exodus is figured as the Puritan exodus from England or the exodus from bondage to freedom that is the dynamic of the American Revolution. But this liberatory exodus of 1776—the communal philology of word and act that is the Declaration of Independence—is complemented by the imperatives of the Constitution: the pursuit of a more perfect union. Swede seeks for himself and Dawn both freedom from the past—he actively dissents against its restraints, its resentments, the grip of history—and the harmony of a more perfect union. He likes the dream of his future life in

Old Rimrock better than the history of his past in Newark, however much his past at Weequahic High, as a star athlete, and Dawn's past, as Miss New Jersey, had its moments of glory, which Swede—and certainly Dawn—seem more willing to forget than Nathan Zuckerman.

The struggle of American democracy since the Revolutionary War has always been the struggle of sons against fathers, against patriarchal authority, but ironically done in the name of the ideals of the father, whether it be God the father, the higher law, or the intent of the letter of the law of the Founding Fathers or the spirit of 1776. America always seems to go postal—or berserk—when the letter becomes dead, whether those letters be the petitions of colonists to England for reform (provoking Jefferson's complaint in his letter to the world, the Declaration, that England had become deaf to the voice of justice and consanguinity) or the letter of the law that Frederick Douglass damns as dead in his "What to the Slave Is the Fourth of July?" address or the promissory note that Martin Luther King Jr. proclaims as bankrupt in his "I Have a Dream" speech. In *American Pastoral* the letters of Lou and Merry are as dead as the dead letters Bartleby must have seen incessantly when he worked for the Dead Letter Office in Washington D.C., and as dead as the spirit of charity and love and the pursuit of a more perfect union in the Wall Street world of Bartleby's New York City in 1855 or Gordon Gekko's Manhattan of the 1980s or the late 1960s Newark, New Jersey of Swede Levov and the Washington D.C. of Lou and Merry Levov in *American Pastoral*. Swede's vision of Old Rimrock is J. Hector St. John de Crèvecoeur's third letter in *Letters from an American Farmer* updated: "Here," in this new world, Crèvecoeur beholds, a place of "substantial villages, extensive fields, an immense country filled with decent houses, good roads, orchards, meadows, and bridges," and while Swede inevitably must see in the 1960s what Crèvecoeur did not see in America in the 1780s—"no great manufacturers employing thousands, no great refinements of luxury" and the "rich and poor are not so far removed from each other as they are in Europe"—he too feels that this pastoral place of Old Rimrock is an "Alma Mater," where people are received in her lap and "melted into a new race of men," a people free from the resentments and social hierarchies of the old world.[21] Lou and Merry Levov, on the other hand, send to Washington, D.C. in their letters the messages of Herman Melville's stories such as *Mardi*, *Moby-Dick*, *Benito Cereno*, *The Confidence-Man*: prophetic denunciations and warnings and lamentations and calls of awakening for a ship of state misgoverned, heading toward shipwreck. But the fate of their reception is to be unread, unheard, undelivered, as misunderstood or neglected as the petitions and protests the radicals in the colonies sent to King George III and Parliament, provoking the "shot heard round the world" that echoes again in the "indigenous American berserk" of the bomb Merry plants in the Old Rimrock post office whose explosion is heard round America.

So far, in most of New Jersey literature of the post–World War II era, the story of the city has been written by authors of a hyphenated identity. "In my neighborhood," Susanne Antonetta writes of Elizabeth, "we had ricks, spicks, micks, nips, jigs, chinks, ricans, hicans. And of course niggers and the much more common mooleys, another corruption of *melanzana*. Negotiating ethnic names was a precise skill and one we picked up early. We kids all used them, often of ourselves, and other than the really loaded *kike* and *nigger*, none were off limits."²² In Brookside, there was, in my memory, coming of age from 1960 to 1971, no such negotiation of ethnic names, even on the Mendham Township school playground. The nicknames—Weasel, Turtle, Igor—were cruel, but not ethnic based. In a place of such racial homogeneity, the ethnic slurs were saved for people outside of Brookside, and their most common slur—referring to one neighborhood in Brookside as the "redneck" section—was based on class, not ethnicity. The primary hierarchy boys and girls made on the playground was an atavistic ranking: boys ranked on athletic skill and girls on looks.

Swede was right in his hope that the world of Old Rimrock would be a place where the resentments and divisions of ethnicity that frictioned people off against each other in the city of Newark would be forgotten or not pronounced and that this new world would be the melting pot imagined by Crèvecoeur, the frictions of the old world giving way to the fusions in the crucible of the new world. The social pressures of this crucible, the pressure that demanded fusion, is the pressure that is felt most not by Swede, who spent his weekdays in Newark, but by Dawn, and, in particular, by Merry. Merry's story by her own telling is the most unwritten story in *American Pastoral*: she seems to have intuited during her coming of age, or to have learned in the hallways of her school, what Lou warns his son, Swede: there are haters out there. There is racism and greed and a tacit snobbery out there. There is pretense out there. There is a cover-up out there, in Old Rimrock, resonant with the cover-ups in 1960s Washington, D.C. This ugly side of Old Rimrock—the noir side, the intolerant side, the side covered up by an aesthetic of politeness and a politics of harmony—gets blown apart in the novel not

by the bomb planted by Merry but by the verbal gre-
nades thrown at this world by Swede's father, Lou, and
his brother, Jerry, and in a quieter way by the tour of
Morris County that Bucky Robinson gives Swede.

The revelation of the anti-pastoral in the midst of a most
fervent dream for the pastoral is the dialectic of *American
Pastoral*, as it was before of F. Scott Fitzgerald's *Great
Gatsby*. If *The Great Gatsby* is the classic, paradigmatic
example of this story in the first part of the twentieth
century, then Roth's *American Pastoral* is the classic, paradigmatic example of this story at the end of the twentieth century: its contemporary counterpart. Swede has
some Rip, Natty, and Huck in him, and he is something
of a James Gatz aspiring to be Jay Gatsby, and *American
Pastoral* is Roth aspiring to overcome *The Great Gatsby* by
giving us a pastoral that is less melodious, more dissonant,
more raucous, even more explosive. (Catherine Roth Pierpont notes at the end of her biographical study of Roth
that Roth sometimes "quotes the last lines of *The Great
Gatsby*, but admits that he has some reservations about the
book: 'It's a bit melodious for my taste.'"[23]). Jay Gatsby was
a nobody from nowhere, and he became enough of a somebody, with the millions he made by hook or by crook, to
have a chance to win over Daisy, which Meyer Wolfsheim,
a Jew, could never have done, no matter how much money
he had obtained from fixing the World Series. Swede
becomes a somebody from a place that he (and then Roth)
helped make a somewhere, a star athlete at Weequahic
High in Newark, and he marries Miss New Jersey, and the
colonial stone house in that green world, which he saw on
a trip out to the Morristown area, becomes his green light,
his Daisy, more so than Dawn, or what he loves the most—
the Daisy of Swede's romantic passion—is the freedom

promised him by a future that he anticipates as much as Gatsby: the "future that was simply to have unrolled out of the solid American past, out of each generation's getting smarter—smarter for knowing the inadequacies and limitations of the generations before—out of each new generation's breaking away from the parochialism a little further, out of the desire to go the limit in America with your rights, forming yourself as an ideal person who gets rid of the traditional Jewish habits and attitudes, who frees himself of the pre-America insecurities and the old, constraining obsessions so as to live unapologetically as an equal among equals" (p. 85).

So we beat on, voices against the current, borne back ceaselessly into the way America has been imagined, with Roth echoing the conclusion of *The Great Gatsby*, or we flow along, voices in the stream, carried down the river, over the falls, echoing William Carlos Williams's *Paterson*—"the city / the man, an identity—it can't be / otherwise"—and Allen Ginsberg's "Garden State": "It used to be, farms, / stone houses on green lawns / a wooded hill to play Jungle Camp. . . . Then came the mafia, alcohol / highways / garbage dumped in marshes, real / estate, World War II, money / flowed thru Nutley, bulldozers."[24] Ginsberg continues with his catalogue of the snakes in the garden who brought about the fall: "Einstein invented atom bombs / in Princeton, television antennae / sprung over West Orange—lobotomies performed in Greystone State Hospital" (p. 726). Ginsberg's mother was institutionalized in Greystone, the "lunatic" asylum, a few miles from the center of Morristown and the center of Brookside. Ginsberg was born in Newark, raised in Paterson, influenced by Williams, and his poem, like *American Pastoral*, is a story of a fall from the garden world perpetrated by the human world juxtaposed against the harmony of the falls of rivers and streams in the natural world. If *American Pastoral* is our great New Jersey novel, Williams's *Paterson* and Ginsberg's "Garden State" are the great New Jersey poems. Just add Bruce Springsteen for the soundtrack and *Harold and Kumar Go to White Castle* and *The Station Agent* and *Paterson* for the movies.

But there is a side of Brookside that beats against the current of New Jersey literature in general and goes against the flow of Williams's *Paterson* and Ginsberg's "Garden State" in particular. Ginsberg writes of "Old graveyards behind churches / on grassy knolls" and of "Erie Railroad / bridges' Checkerboard underpass / signs, paint fading, remain / Reminds me of a time pond's pure / water was green, drink or swim" (p. 726). Bill Orcutt takes Swede Levov to the graveyard beyond a church on a grassy knoll in Mendham, New Jersey. The rain that falls on the roof of the church, as Orcutt tells Swede, goes on one side into the Raritan and the other side into the Passaic. Brookside is at the headwaters of both rivers, and kids can still walk the streams of Brookside, both Harmony Brook and Dismal Brook, and enter them and go chest deep in the pool of water under the falls of Dismal Brook, and see and feel unpolluted water, as pure maybe as it was in the 1960s and purer than it probably was in the late nineteenth century when these brooks served the needs of a small industrial town, making possible its grist mills and saw mills and tanneries.

The Station Agent is in part an elegy to something that has passed—the railroad—as well as a quiet ode to invisible small communities and the bonds forged by small talk and the kindness of being a good neighbor (as it unveils the ugliness in a small town too). The lead character in the

story, the station agent, is played by the actor Peter Din-
klage, who grew up in Brookside on East Main Street,
where he might have imagined the time when a railroad—
the Rock-a-Bye-Baby—ran through the center of the
town, just beyond the fence of the baseball field. The writer
and director of *The Station Agent*, Thomas McCarthy,
grew up in nearby New Providence, New Jersey. For some
of the locations in the movie, he uses places at the end of
the line of the old Morris and Essex Railroad, now the Erie
Lackawanna, such as Dover, Rockaway Township, and
Lake Hopatcong. The movie gives us a rich sense of the
particular: it is not the usual formulaic Hollywood movie,
and besides being the one movie (or the best movie) that
takes us out to rural northwestern New Jersey (after its
opening in a model train hobby shop in Hoboken), it has
a uniqueness—as does *American Pastoral*—in how it
makes these places unmarked by any exit off the Turnpike
or Parkway so iconic.

Williams's *Paterson* opens with the lines, "To make a
start, / out of particulars / and make them general."[25] The
particulars of Brookside are made general, indeed mythic
of America, by Roth, just as Williams makes the particulars of *Paterson* mythic, and Ginsberg does the same with
the particulars of history from Morris and Essex Counties
in "Garden State": "They threw eggs at Norman Thomas
the Socialist speaker / in Newark Military Park, the police
/ stood by & laughed. Used to murder / silk strikers on
Mill St. in the twenties. . . . Here in Boonton they made
cannonballs / for Washington" (p. 727).[26] Einstein invent-
ing the atom bomb, eggs thrown at Norman Thomas,
strikers murdered, lobotomies performed: these particulars are anti-pastoral. But Ginsberg at the end of "Garden

State" leaves us singing "old springtime music / on Greystone State Mental Hospital Lawn" (p. 727). This is the juxtaposition of Swede's vision of Old Rimrock, the song he sings of this garden world, and the "indigenous American berserk" of Merry: it is New Jersey and America at once as pastoral and anti-pastoral, a place that is beautiful-berserk. The particulars of this place make it at once fallen and unfallen. Yet however fallen it is, it is also a place that beats against the current, against the flow of New Jersey history. Brookside is not a place where they paved paradise and put up a parking lot, a mall, a corporate headquarters. Instead, this is a place transformed by the combined power of wealth and the entrepreneurship of developers and town hall civic activism from a former small industrial town into a pastoral retreat, a paradise regained, a fresh, green breast of a new world kept old, an alma mater I love, but, *pace* Swede and Nathan, I must also insist: this place is not unreprehensible.

Acknowledgments

As a favorite archive for this study, I use the details of Brookside's history both remembered and researched by me, including stories told to me by my mom who served as the assistant township clerk for Mendham Township and a secretary for its police department. My mom's love for this town, equaling if not surpassing the joy Swede Levov first takes in Old Rimrock, is a primary inspiration for this book. She and my father, who served the town as its elected tax assessor and on its planning board for more than twenty years, inspired me with their own civic commitment to believe what is inscribed in the Tom Bradley room of Los Angeles's city hall—"the city exists for the good life"—and a corollary: the good life consists in serving the city. Brookside is an icon of a small town, and it was the first polis to shape my identity. I have lived in major cities—New Haven, New York City, San Francisco, Los Angeles—ever since leaving for college, but I will always be, deep inside of me, a kid from Brookside, born and raised on a dead-end dirt road called Stoney Hill Road in the middle of this small town of 3,500 residents in the 1960s.

Here I want to single out for special acknowledgment several of the voices from Brookside and my life beyond

Brookside that contributed to the shaping of this book. First from my elementary school is Mrs. McGill, my seventh-grade language arts teacher for whom I wrote for the first time an essay about Stoney Hill Road. From my high school, Pingry, I give special thanks to Tom Behr, my freshman English teacher who encouraged me to go into print in a freshman newspaper with an essay I wrote for his class about Stoney Hill Road, and Miller Bugliari, a biology teacher and my varsity soccer coach who exemplifies for me the significance of always understanding our local history. Special for me as well from my life in Brookside are my closest friend growing up, Fred Hartley, and Sam Tufts, my baseball coach for Little League and Babe Ruth teams. My dear friend from college and graduate school and Los Angeles, Rob Watson, a professor of English at the University of California, Los Angeles, first told me I had to read *American Pastoral* and commented on an early draft as did our mutual friend from college, Fred Cantor.

I have had the chance to share memories of Brookside in the 1960s with my first wife, Martha Gillis, who grew up in this town too, not far from the post office and across the street on Hilltop Circle Drive from Jerry Bohrer, a graduate with Philip Roth of Weequahic High. My oldest memory of her is marching in the Brookside Fourth of July parade dressed in a flapper style from the 1920s behind a banner evoking late 1960s feminism that read "We've Come a Long Way Baby." Her perspective on Brookside has helped me appreciate the dissonant voice of the character Merry Levov. Thanks to our visits home to Brookside with our three kids to see our parents (who remained living in Brookside all their lives), I have had the chance to experience with our children—Sarah, Britta, and

Elisabeth—the deep joy we each took in Dismal Harmony, the Brookside Pond and the Fourth of July parade. Elisabeth guided me sometimes after long night shifts as a nurse through preparing images for publication. I have also loved the chances to share Brookside with my wife, Lupe, and her youngest daughter, Alexia, including the joy of taking Alexia, at a young age, for a swim at Brookside Beach, which remains one of her favorite earliest memories.

I thank my colleagues in the University of Southern California's English Department, Joseph Dane and David St. John, for their long friendship and support for this project and my two neighbors on the fourth floor of Taper Hall, Rick Berg and John Carlos Rowe, for listening to me when I showed them my photos of the Brookside post office alongside the cover of *American Pastoral*, with John encouraging me to write about it all.

I love libraries, and the Mendham Township Library in the municipal building is a first and enduring love. For many years, it was run mostly by volunteers, and my mom was one of them. I thank all the volunteers who ever served to sustain this library as part of the small, strong heart of my hometown.

No matter how much I write about Brookside, the two readers who will understand it best are my sister, Gwenda, and my brother, Gregory: In my heart, we will always be together, as we are on the Molly Pitcher float my father built for the Brookside Fourth of July parade in 1957. This book is for them and, especially, in memoriam, for my mom and dad, deservedly grand marshals of the Brookside Fourth of July parade in 1994.

Notes

Prologue

1   William Carlos Williams, "Author's Note" to *Paterson* (New York: New Directions, 1963), n.p.

2   Philip Roth, quoted in Paul Gray, "Novelist: Philip Roth," *Time Magazine*, July 9, 2001, and as cited by Ben Siegel, "Introduction: Reading Philip Roth: Facts and Fancy, Fiction and Autobiography," *Turning Up the Flame: Philip Roth's Later Novels*, ed. Jay Halio and Ben Siegel (Newark: University of Delaware Press, 2005), 28.

3   Michael Kimmage, *In History's Grip: Philip Roth's Newark Trilogy* (Stanford, CA: Stanford University Press, 2012), 4. The literary criticism of *American Pastoral* is extensive, befitting its Pulitzer Prize and its high place in Roth's own judgment about his work. My own approach is not to emphasize how and where I agree or disagree with the criticism of other scholars on this novel but to study it in relation to the history of a place—specifically, the relationship between Roth's Old Rimrock and Brookside as other scholars have done with studying Roth's Newark in relation to the history of Newark—as well as its relationship to the literature of New Jersey. For me, a key guide to studying the history of criticism of *American Pastoral* are the essays by David Brauner, Andrew Gordon, and Jennifer Glaser in Deborah Shostak, ed. *Philip Roth* (London: Continuum, 2011).

4   F. Scott Fitzgerald, *The Great Gatsby* (New York: Scribner, 1925). As I discuss in part III, *American Pastoral* revisits this conclusion near its own ending.

5 Mark Shechner, a scholar from Newark, calls Old Rimrock a "mythic rural paradise" in *Up Society's Ass, Copper: Rereading Philip Roth* (Madison: University of Wisconsin Press, 2003), 155, and "a mythic exurban retreat" in his essay "Roth's American Trilogy" in *The Cambridge Companion to Philip Roth* (Cambridge: Cambridge University Press, 2007), 142. Thomas R. Hummel in *A Journey Through Literary America* (Napa, CA: Val De Grace Books, 2009) features Roth in an eleven-page section entitled: "Newark & Mendham, New Jersey," pp. 236–247. But Hummel misidentifies the town and location for Old Rimrock and its post office. In his book, there are five photos of Newark, including one of Weequahic High School, and one page and one photo and one column of text devoted to Mendham. Here is an excerpt:

> Old Rimrock, with its combination of post office and general store, is a fictional locale. But there are some who hold that Roth, a meticulous researcher, based Old Rimrock on Mendham, a town at the edges of New Jersey's horse country. Though it is much busier now than in its fictional incarnation, when the Swede used to walk into town with his loping athletic stride to collect the mail and chat with the proprietors of the general store, Mendham still trails off into countryside and possesses a combination post office and general store. A black-and-white photograph of innocent-looking young men and women posing outside just such an establishment appears on the cover of the first edition of *American Pastoral*. (p. 244)

The book then includes a photo of the "combination General Store and Post Office in Mendham, thought to be the inspiration for Old Rimrock" (pp. 244–245). But the photo Hummel includes is of the Ralston General Store, now a museum, and not the Brookside post office. The town that he describes as now "much busier" is Mendham Borough, not Brookside. The Brookside post office is still in Brookside, looking so much like it does on the original front cover of the novel, and the town is no busier than it was in the 1960s. Blake Bailey in *Philip Roth: The Biography* (New York: Norton, 2021) makes his own mistake of detail when he writes that when John T. Cunningham, a historian of New Jersey, was touring Mendham, New Jersey to help Roth find an "idyllic setting" for Old Rimrock, Roth spotted the photo used on the front cover of the first edition of *American Pastoral* "on the wall of a general store in tiny Brookside" and "asked the owner whether he could borrow it" (p. 609). At the time, the building with the photo used for the front cover was solely a post office, not a general store with an owner. Roth, unlike Hummel and Bailey, is a "meticulous researcher." The description of Old Rimrock in *American Pastoral* is as grounded in fact as his descriptions of Newark (or almost as close). Bailey also confirms that it was Cunningham, who was born in Newark and raised in Brookside, "who thought the area perfect for the idyllic setting of 'Old Rimrock' . . ." (p. 609). Cunningham now has a stretch of Patriot's Path near the center of Brookside and his childhood home named after him: The John T. Cunningham Trail. (Just as Cunningham's 1966 history of Newark served Roth as a guide, his histories of New Jersey—as well as personal conversations—seemed to have served Roth as a guide to Morris County and Brookside.)

6 Williams, "Author's Note" to *Paterson*, n.p.

7 Williams, "Author's Note" to *Paterson*, n.p.

8 Census Reporter. The race and ethnicity for Brookside (population, 1,387) is currently reported as White 85.0 percent, Black 1.0 percent, Asian 2.0 percent, Hispanic 6.0 percent, Native 0.0 percent, two or more races 5.0 percent. The race and ethnicity for Mendham Township (population, 5998) is reported as White 85.0 percent, Black 1.0 percent, Asian 4.0 percent, Hispanic 4.0 percent, two or more races 4.0 percent, Other 3.0 percent.

9 In 1958, fifteen people joined together to purchase land to form what became the Mendham Golf & Tennis Club. The course opened for play in 1961 with six holes and became an eighteen-hole course in 1969. A short history of the club is available on its website: https://www.mendhamgolfandtennis.com/.

1. The Office of Letters and the Bomb

1 In the 1960s, there was a cost-saving movement by the U.S. Postal Service to eliminate the Brookside post office and deliver the mail directly to driveway mailboxes as was done with all other zip codes serving Mendham Township, but enough townspeople protested this change to nullify it.

2   F. Scott Fitzgerald, *The Great Gatsby* (New York: Scribner's Sons, 1925), 182. The phrase "fresh, green breast" is from the famous conclusion of the novel. The writers mentioned form part of a core group of contributors in American letters to the development and critique of the pastoral tradition in American culture that now includes Roth.

2. Fourth of July Parade

1   See https://www.mendhamtownship.org/home/news /grandest-little-hometown-parade-america-wants-you.

2   Christopher Merrill, *Workbook* (Santa Fe: Teal Press, 1988), 13.

3   Steven Cramer, *The World Book* (Providence, RI: Copper Beech Press, 1992), 34–35. Note: Merrill's poem dates the parade in 1970 and Cramer's poem in 1968. In his memoir, *Self-Portrait with Dogwood* (San Antonio: Trinity University Press, 2017), Merrill provides a compelling prose account of this incident and its context.

4   Ronald Reagan, "Second Inaugural Address," 1985, https:// avalon.law.yale.edu/20th_century/reagan2.asp.

5   Tony Kushner, "American Things," in *Thinking about the Longstanding Problem of Virtue: Essays, a Play, Two Poems, and a Prayer* (Theater Communications Group, 1995).

6   The phrase is from Thomas Jefferson's draft of the Declaration of Independence in *Writings* (New York: Library of America, 1984), 22.

7   Richard Slotkin, *Regeneration through Violence: The Mythology of the American Frontier, 1600–1800* (Middletown, CT: Wesleyan University Press, 1974). His other two books in the trilogy are *The Fatal Environment: The Myth of the Frontier in the Age of Industrialization, 1800–1890* (New York: Macmillan, 1985) and *Gunfighter Nation: Myth of the Frontier in Twentieth Century* (New York: Atheneum, 1992). Jill Lepore, "Battleground America: One Nation, Under the Gun," *New Yorker*, April 23, 2012.

8   In *Representative Words: Politics, Literature, and the American Language, 1776–1865* (Cambridge: Cambridge University Press, 1992), I devote twenty pages to Thomas Paine in a chapter called "The Language of Revolution: Combating Misrepresentation with the Pen and the Tongue." Roth included Howard Fast's *Citizen Tom Paine* in a list of the

fifteen books that influenced him the most, with Fast's book
at the top of the list in terms of the chronology of his reading.
See https://www.openculture.com/2018/05/philip-roth-rip
-creates-a-list-of-the-15-books-that-influenced-him-most.html.

9   Nathaniel Hawthorne, "My Kinsman, Major Molineux," in
Nathaniel Hawthorne: Tales and Sketches (New York: Library
of America, 1982), 84, 86.

3. Indigenous American Berserk

1   Philip Roth, *The Dying Animal* (New York: Vintage, 2001),
59, 61. Peter Mancall in *The Trials of Thomas Morton: An
Anglican Lawyer, His Puritan Foes, and the Battle for New
England* (New Haven, CT: Yale University Press, 2019) uses as
its epigraph the passage from *The Dying Animal* pondering
the direction New England and America would have taken if
Morton's mission, not Bradford's, had prevailed.

2   For the significance of New Jersey in the American Revolution, see Maxine N. Lurie, *Taking Sides in Revolutionary New
Jersey* (New Brunswick, NJ: Rutgers University Press, 2022).

3   For an illuminating study of the significance of the violence
and trauma of the American Revolution as a context for the
events of *American Pastoral*, see Aimee Pozorski, "American
Pastoral and the Traumatic Ideals of Democracy," chapter 3 in
*Roth and Trauma: The Problem of History in the Later Works
(1995–2010)* (New York: Continuum, 2011).

4   For Morristown's importance in the Revolutionary War, see
John T. Cunningham, *The Uncertain Revolution: Washington &
the Continental Army at Morristown* (West Creek, NJ:
Cormorant Publishing, 2007) and William Hazelgrove,
*Morristown: The Darkest Winter of the Revolutionary War and
the Plot to Kidnap George Washington* (Guilford, CT: Lyons
Press, 2021).

5   I have something of a "lover's quarrel" with *American
Pastoral*, and the quarrel side of my relationship is best
addressed by John Carlos Rowe in "Neoliberalism and the
U.S. Literary Canon: The Example of Philip Roth," chapter 8 in *Afterlives of Modernism: Liberalism, Transnationalism,
and Political Critique* (Hanover, NH: Dartmouth College
Press, 2011). Rowe argues how, despite Roth's embrace of
liberal tolerance, he "stereotypes these extremes": "In *American*

Pastoral, the New Left is reduced to the madness of Swede's daughter, Merry, a Weatherman bomber who kills four innocent people, and to Roth's caricature of Angela Davis as a revolutionary committed to the destruction of U.S. democracy" (pp. 190–191).

6　Ronald Sullivan, "War Protestors Meet Opposition," *New York Times*, September 6, 1970, p. 8.

7　I searched out stories about the Fourth of July parade in Brookside on the Internet. The favorite one I found was about plans to make the theme for the 2012 Fourth of July the 1960s. Here is the description of the theme of the parade from an article written by Phil Garber in the June 18, 2012, edition of the *Observer-Tribune* entitled, "It's back to the '60s for Brookside July 4 Parade": "Tie dyed shirts, shaggy hair, peace signs and the sounds of the Beatles will be in vogue, if only for one day, at this year's Brookside July 4 parade. The only thing missing will be that pervasive, sweet scent of illicit drugs that was emblematic of the years of turning on, tuning in and dropping out. 'Brookstock' will be theme as marchers, floats and bands will focus on a theme from the halcyon years of peace and love of the baby boomers"; see https://www .newjerseyhills.com/observer-tribune/news/it-s-back-to-the-60s -for-brookside-july-4-parade/article_1dc26b88-b976-11e1-8d7a - 0014bcf887a.html. Missing of course will also be any representation of the violence and tragedies of the Vietnam War that Merry protests in *American Pastoral* and all that the black coffin and its mirror represented at the July 4, 1969, parade.

4. Fig Leaf

1　Herman Melville, *Billy Budd, Sailor* in *Melville* (New York: Library of America, 1984), 1430.

5. Walled Garden

1　U.S. Census Bureau, Mendham Township, https://www .census.gov/quickfacts/mendhamtownshipmorriscountynewj ersey.

2　The page on the official Mendham Township website giving the historical perspective on Brookside and its origins and concluding in its celebration of being a place free from "satanic mills" has been removed from the town's official website since

late 2021. It can be found in the "Historical Overview" section
for the town on the Mendham Township School District
website: https://www.mendhamtwp.org/community.

3   Mendham Township School District, https://www
    .mendhamtwp.org/community.

4   Text of historical marker on East Main Street near the
    Community Club.

5   Morris County, NJ Website, https://www.morriscountynj
    .gov/Departments/Planning-and-Preservation/Cultural
    -Resources-Survey/Historic-Maps.

6   Department of the Interior, National Register of Historic
    Places Registration Form for Brookside, section 7, page 1,
    1996, https://npgallery.nps.gov/GetAsset/78d1e543-4bb2
    -4b7a-8870-40b7fa96bdb4. This form was primarily authored
    by Janet W. Foster, a scholar and professor of historical
    preservation. For an early history of Mendham Township when
    the population of Brookside is listed as 187, see S. B. Axtell,
    "Mendham Township," in *The History of Morris County,
    New Jersey, with Illustrations and Biographical Sketches of
    Prominent Citizens and Pioneers* (New York: W. W. Munsell &
    Co., 1882).

7   Department of the Interior. National Register of Historic
    Places Registration Form for Brookside (1996), Section 7, p. 1.

8   Department of the Interior. National Register of Historic
    Places Registration Form for Brookside (1996), Section 8, p. 4.

9   Department of the Interior. National Register of Historic
    Places Registration Form for Brookside. 1996. Section 8, p. 8.
    On May 29, 2023, the Mendham Township Historic Preserva-
    tion Committee inaugurated a new website (historicmend-
    hamtwp.com) dedicated to telling and documenting the
    history of Mendham Township. The website divides itself into
    the following sections: "About," "History," "Places" ("Historic
    Districts," "Architecture"), "People" ("Founding Families,"
    "Community & Business Leaders"), and "Industry" ("Mills,"
    "Shops," "Mining," "Farming," "Factories," "Government").
    The "History" tab provides an annotated and illustrated
    timeline of the history of Mendham Township from the time
    of the Leni Lenape into the twentieth century. This section
    includes an array of old photos and an interactive map of
    Mendham Township with a color-coded outline of each of its
    historic districts: Brookside, Ralston, Washington Valley,
    Combs Hollow, and Tempe Wick. A cursor can be

manipulated to locate and travel along any road in the township. This site is still a work in progress with sections needing to be further defined and information added.

10 This brief sketch of the history of Dismal Harmony and Harmony Village is pieced together from information in chapters II and III in Martha G. Hopler, Edward W. Roseller, and Wallace G. West, *The Mendhams*, a history published by the Mayor's Tercentenary Committee under the sponsorship of the Township Committee of the Township of Mendham (1964), based in part on a history in typescript by Frank Dean, a township clerk for Brookside, written in 1946, entitled "Notes on the Early History of Mendham Township." I have also drawn upon research done by Sarah Dean Link, a Mendham Township librarian and member of its Environmental Commission, shared with me by my mother.

11 A description of the events for the Fourth of July celebration in 2019 suggests that civic pride measured by this celebration continues. The theme for the 2019 parade was "Brookside: The Happiest Little Place on Earth." For the full text of this announcement, see Katie Kausch, *The Patch,* June 21, 2019, https://patch.com/new-jersey/mendham-chester/mendhams -annual-4th-july-parade-brookside-back-2019. One measure of change in the town would be the elimination from the schedule of events contests in fire ladder raising, skeet shooting, horseshoes, the frog jump, and the turtle race.

12 *Forbes Magazine*, "America's Most Expensive Zip Codes," August 27, 2009, https://www.forbes.com/2009/08/26/most -expensive-zip-codes-lifestyle-real-estate-zip_full-list.html.

13 Thanks to the librarians of the Mendham Borough Library, I obtained an article from their archives written by John T. Cunningham in 1965 entitled, "Mendham: My Home," that was published in the November 1965 issue of *Crossroads Magazine*. Cunningham gives an affectionate portrait of Mendham Borough including the Hilltop Presbyterian Church that William Orcutt highlights in his tour for Swede Levov. But the title is misleading. Cunningham's home, as he reveals, was Brookside, not Mendham: "For a boy growing up in Brookside, as I did, Mendham was a metropolis" (p. 10). Cunningham makes the poignant distinction: Brookside, unlike Mendham, had no business district. Instead, it cultivated the aura of being a rural village—a pastoral place.

14 Robyn Magalit Rodriguez, *In Lady Liberty's Shadow: The Politics of Race and Immigration in New Jersey* (New Brunswick, NJ: Rutgers University Press, 2017) studies the politics of racism and xenophobia in suburban towns in New Jersey including a section on Morristown, giving a historical profile of the town going back to the Revolution and looking closely at the racial fears that manifested in this county seat post-9/11. My study suggests that such racial fears in Morristown and Brookside have a long history, with the late 1960s, like post-9/11, a time of their intensification.

15 Lizabeth Cohen, *A Consumers' Republic: The Politics of Mass Consumption in Postwar America* (New York: Vintage, 2004), 199.

16 Cohen, *A Consumers' Republic*, 213.

17 Howard Gillette Jr. in his essay "Suburbanization and the Decline of the Cities: Toward an Uncertain Future," in *New Jersey: A History of the Garden State*, ed. Maxine N. Lurie and Richard Veit (New Brunswick, NJ: Rutgers University Press, 2012), 264–285, gives us the other shoe dropping in relation to Cohen's account of the suburbanization of New Jersey—and something that Swede is blind to in his vision of Old Rimrock and that the history of zoning in Mendham Township exemplifies: how "race and class differentiations were institutionalized by local land use decisions" (p. 266). "Most important," Gillette writes, "was the power of each community to pass zoning regulations that prohibited undesirable practices, including the introduction of lower-cost residential properties that might attract lower-income residents. By requiring minimum lot sizes in order to keep prices high . . . communities could maximize property values while minimizing social costs" (pp. 266–267). He adds, "Such exclusionary zoning, as it came to be called, helped some suburbs, if not all, maintain their distance from urban influences" (p. 267).

18 Donald Reilly, "Religious Freedom Is My Ultimate Goal," *New Yorker*, June 3, 1974.

6. All Babel Breaks Loose

1 Jefferson, *Writings*, 23.

2 Patricia Limerick, *The Legacy of Conquest: The Unbroken Past of the American West* (New York: Norton, 1987). Limerick

articulates another version of this dream vision at the end of *The Legacy of Conquest*. In her vision, the peoples of America studying the common ground they have occupied including through violence and dispossession of others come to know each other through a shared historical understanding of this common ground (including its tragedies).

7. Inside the Territory

1   Thomas Gray, *Elegy Written in a Country Churchyard* (Mount Vernon, New York: Peter Pauper Press, 1947), 9.

2   In his own remarks at his eightieth birthday celebration, Roth declared, "This passion for specificity, for the hypnotic materiality, of the world one is in, is at the heart of the task to which every American novelist has been enjoined since Melville and his whale and Twain and his river: to discover the most arresting, evocative verbal depiction for every last American thing." See Philip Roth's own contribution to *Philip Roth at 80: A Celebration* (New York: The Library of America, 2014), 53–54. Sean Wilentz in remarks on Roth at this event commented too on his "acute sense of history" and his "concern for exactness." See Sean Wilentz, "An Acute Sense of History," in *Philip Roth Personal Library* (Newark, NJ: Newark Public Library, 2022), 29.

3   Toni Morrison, *The Nobel Lecture in Literature* (New York: Knopf, 1993).

4   In chapter 3 of *Representative Words*, I trace this tradition of protesting the "corruption of language" from Thucydides through Emerson to George Orwell's "Politics and the English Language" (1946) and Kenneth Burke's *Rhetoric of Motives* (1950), a tradition to which we need to add Roth's *Our Gang* (1971).

5   For the concept of "regeneration through violence," see Slotkin's trilogy on the myth of the frontier cited previously.

6   Cramer, *The World Book*.

8. Harmony

1   See John T. Cunningham, "Morris: Iron Backbone," in *This is New Jersey*, 4th ed. (New Brunswick, NJ: Rutgers University Press, 2001).

2   See the conclusion of Limerick, *The Legacy of Conquest*.

9. Dissonance

1 This section on Mt. Freedom and its relationship to Swede's identity—and Roth's own relationship to his Jewish identity—needs to be read in the light of Brett Ashley Kaplan's excellent study, *Jewish Anxiety in the Novels of Philip Roth* (London: Bloomsbury Academic, 2016).

2 Christopher Merrill, "Dismal Harmony," *Third Coast*, no. 21 (Fall 2005).

3 Michael Rosenthal, *The Character Factory: Baden-Powell and the Origins of the Boy Scout Movement* (New York: Pantheon, 1986).

4 Patricia Ard and Michael Aaron Rockland, *The Jews of New Jersey: A Pictorial History* (New Brunswick, NJ: Rutgers University Press, 2002), 47–58. Even closer to Brookside than Camp Nordland, the town of Chester, which bordered Mendham Township on its Ralston side, had a large gathering of the Ku Klux Klan in 1926 at its Chester Federated Church. Photos of this gathering can be found in the Photograph and Image Collection of the Caroline Rose Foster North Jersey History Collection & Genealogy Center that is part of the Morristown and Morris County Library.

5 For a short history of Mt. Freedom in photographs, see Linda B. Forgosh, "Mount Freedom: Farewell to Little Broadway," chapter 4 of *Jews of Morris County* (Charleston, SC: Arcadia Press, 2006).

6 Karen Kominsky, "The Rise and Decline of Resorts in Mt. Freedom," *New Jersey Hills*, October 13, 2005.

7 Michael M. Meyer, ed. *Joachim Prinz, Rebellious Rabbi* (Bloomington: Indiana University Press, 2008), 186.

8 Dana Johnson uses this line to describe Henry Huntington in her story, "The Story of Biddy Mason," in her collection of stories, *In the Not Quite Dark: Stories* (Berkeley, CA: Counterpoint, 2016).

9 Frances Fitzgerald, *Fire in the Lake* (Boston; Little, Brown, 1972).

10. Counterfactual

1 *Jenkins v. Twp. of Morris School Dist. and Bd. of Ed.* (https://law.justia.com/cases/new-jersey/supreme-court/1971/58-n-j-483-0.html). The decision is a fascinating time capsule to read for the statistics regarding the markedly different

demographics of wealth and ethnicity between Morristown and Morris Township and for the language—progressive and noble then, but problematical now (a case of white savior rhetoric)—for the benefits of integration.

2   But a newspaper account in the *New York Times* at the time looked at it with no rose-tinted glasses: "The merger of two school districts to achieve racial integration here is proceeding painfully, inexorably and, despite the fact that similar efforts elsewhere are floundering." Quoted from "In Morris, a Painful Schools Merger," *New York Times*, October 21, 1973. In 2000, Madison was 89.69 percent white and 3 percent African American. Morristown was 68 percent white and 17 percent African American.

3   "Madison Divided on Barber Ruling," *New York Times*, December 18, 1964.

4   Information from Kevin Coughlin, "Remembering One of Morristown's Finest: George Jenkins Sr., a Community Cop for Turbulent Times," MorristownGreen.com, January 10, 2017.

5   In 2018, the Morristown and Morris Township Library hosted an exhibit that explored over 300 years of race relations between Black and white in Morris County entitled, "The Ties that Bind: How Race Relations Shaped Morris County and New Jersey, 1688–2018." Unfortunately, I have not seen this exhibit, but I would say that just as *American Pastoral* is quiet about Black history and politics in Morris County, it seems as if neither address race relations involving the Latino and Asian and South Asian communities. In Morris County in 2020, the five largest ethnic groups were white (non-Hispanic) 70.5 percent, Asian (non-Hispanic) 10.5 percent, white (Hispanic) 9 percent, Black or African American 3.07 percent. See https://datausa.io/profile/geo/morris-county-nj#:~:text=The%205%20largest%20ethnic%20groups,(Hispanic)%20(2.31%25).

11. On the Dead-End Dirt Road

1   The phrase "quiet babel" of Brookside also applies to the many streams of gossip coursing through the town about affairs. The fall of the marriage of Swede and Dawn into affairs and betrayals has more than its share of historical examples in this era.

2 Merrill, *Self-Portait with Dogwood*.

3 The Pitney family has its own website (pitneyfarm.org) that profiles its family members dating back to the eighteenth century in conjunction with a history of the farm. The profiles include information about education (e.g., Princeton University) and service in the military. The final patriarch of the Pitney farm, Duncan Pitney, after serving in World War II, became an artist. This Pitney family genealogy bears close comparison to the family history William Orcutt gives Swede Levov (pp. 305–306) of his own genealogy.

4 See Linda Prevost, *Snob Zones: Fear, Prejudice, Real Estate* (Boston: Beacon Press, 2013) for a study of such exclusionary practices in a set of New England states.

5 The statistics here draw upon Colleen Day, "Newark before the Comeback: A City Marked by White Flight, Poor Policy," *NJ Spotlight News,* September 9, 2019. https://www.njspotlightnews.org/2019/09/19-09-02-newark-before-the-comeback-a-city-marked-by-white-flight-and-poor-policy/.

6 Cohen, *A Consumers' Republic*, 224.

7 Cohen, *A Consumers' Republic*.

8 Cohen, *A Consumers' Republic*.

12. Brookside Bards

1 Steven Cramer, *Goodbye to the Orchard* (Louisville, KY: Sarabande Books, 2004).

2 Cramer, *The World Book*, 29.

3 Merrill, "Poaching," in *Workbook*, 23.

4 Stockton's "The Story of Tempe Wick" is included in *Stories of New Jersey* (New Brunswick, NJ: Rutgers University Press, 1961).

5 In the second chapter of *Self-Portrait with Dogwood*, entitled "Dismal Harmony," Christopher Merrill gives us his engaging telling of the story of Tempe Wick, updating it from Stockton's account. The story of Jockey Hollow is also at the center of Boyd Wright's novel, *Jockey Hollow: A Novel of the American Revolution* (Bloomington, IN: 1st Books Library, 2003). Wright, a former newspaper editor, lives in Mendham, two miles from Jockey Hollow. This is the ur-story of Mendham Township, just as the story of General Washington's crossing of the Delaware is an ur-story for Revolutionary New Jersey.

13. Brookside against the Current

1 Crèvecoeur, J. Hector St. John de, *Letters from an American Farmer and Sketches of 18th-Century America* (New York: Penguin Books, 1981), 66–105.
2 Fitzgerald, *The Great Gatsby*, 182.
3 Mark Twain, *The Adventures of Huckleberry Finn* (New York: Penguin Books, 2003), 307.
4 Ralph Ellison, *Going to the Territory* (New York: Random House, 1986), 243, and Ralph Ellison, *Shadow and Act* (New York: New American Library, 1966), 42.
5 Tony Kushner, *Thinking about the Longstanding Problem of Virtue: Essays, a Play, Two Poems, and a Prayer* (Theater Communications Group, 1995), 11.
6 Reagan, "Second Inaugural Address."
7 Sacvan Bercovitch, *American Jeremiad* (Madison: University of Wisconsin Press, 1978).

14. NIMBY

1 The Municipal Land Use Law for New Jersey has enabled "historic preservation zoning" since 1986 according to the Historic Preservation Office in the state's Department of Environmental Protection.
2 Bob Ingle and Michael Symons, *Chris Christie: The Inside Story of His Rise to Power* (New York: St. Martin's Press, 2012).
3 For a brief review of some of Christie's politics as a Morris Country freeholder, see also Claire Heininger, "GOP Candidate Chris Christie Launched Political Career as Morris County Freeholder," May 12, 2009, https://www.nj .com/news/2009/05/gop_candidate_chris_christie_l.html.
4 For a perspective on the development of environmental politics in New Jersey in the early 1970s, see Howard L. Green, ed. "Opening Pandora's Box? A Debate on Environmental Policy (1972)," in *Words that Make New Jersey History: A Primary Source Reader* (New Brunswick, NJ: Rutgers University Press, 2009).
5 See the *Observer Tribune News* article, "Taking Pride in Brookside," July 1, 2022, https://www.newjerseyhills.com /observer-tribune/news/taking-pride-in-brookside/image _ccefd64f-a27e-547b-a50a-bfbb3e847e12.html. This Pride

event at the Brookside Beach is now also called Mendham Township's "National Night Out."

15. The Price of Harmony

1 Shechner, *Up Society's Ass*, 168.
2 Herman Melville, *Billy Budd, Sailor*, ed. Harrison Hayford and Merton M. Sealts Jr. (Chicago: University of Chicago Press, 1962), 88.
3 Jefferson, *Writings*, 23.
4 I thank my colleague, John Carlos Rowe, for challenging me to greet Roth's politics in *American Pastoral* less politely thanks to his arguments about the novel in chapter 8 of *Afterlives of Modernism*.

16. The Table of Otherhood and Communion

1 Martin Luther King Jr., *A Testament of Hope: The Essential Writings and Speeches* (New York: Harper, 2003), 217.
2 James Madison, *Notes of Debates in the Federal Convention of 1787 Reported by James Madison*, ed. Adrienne Koch (New York: Norton, 1969), 653–654.
3 Madison, *Notes of Debates*.
4 Ralph Waldo Emerson, *Essays and Lectures* (New York: Library of America, 1983), 408.
5 Emerson, *Essays and Lectures*.
6 Emerson, *Essays and Lectures*.
7 Thomas Pynchon, *The Crying of Lot 49* (New York: Harper, 1966), 118, 82.
8 W. H. Auden, *Secondary Worlds* (New York: Random House, 1968), 134.
9 James Russell Lowell, *The Works of James Russell Lowell*, 10 vols. (Boston: Houghton Mifflin, 1890), VIII: 87.
10 Sherry B. Ortner, *New Jersey Dreaming: Capital, Culture, and the Class of 1958* (Durham, NC: Duke University Press, 2003). Not included around this table are some of the following authors who have lived or set stories in New Jersey but who are less recognized for an association with New Jersey literature: James Fenimore Cooper (Burlington). Rebecca Harding Davis (Manasquan), Bret Harte (Morristown), Mary E. Wilkins Freeman (Metuchen), F. Scott Fitzgerald (Princeton).

More poets with a connection to New Jersey could be part of this gathering including Philip Freneau (Freehold), John Ciardi (Metuchen), C. K. Williams (Newark, Maplewood, Hopewell), Maria Mazziotti Gillan (Paterson).

17. The Community Club and Its Dissidents

1   This statement is quoted from the Brookside Community Club membership form for 2021 (and it does not appear on the 2023 membership form). The Mendham Township Historic Preservation Committee on June 10, 2023, posted on its website (historicmendhamtwp.com) an engaging, very informative history of the Community Club that notes the role of a local entrepreneur, Benjamin Natkins, in the transformation of Brookside in the early 1920s from a place of small industry to a residential community.

2   Pia Masiero, *Philip Roth and the Zuckerman Books: The Making of a Storyworld* (New York: Cambria Press, 2011), chapter 5.

3   Emerson, *Essays and Lectures*, 10.

4   We learn in the novel something else about the reading of Merry: "Dawn had let out a scream. All because of Merry's reading of Karl Marx and Angela Davis!" (p. 158). On a personal note, I wonder what books Merry discovered in the library that not only introduced her to "Algeria" and Marx and Davis but had the effect on her conscience when younger similar to the effect on me of two books I read in 1965 that took me far outside of Brookside and deep into places of social injustice, one of them recommended to me from the school library of Mendham Township Elementary School by Mrs. Clark, my sixth-grade social studies teacher—*An Indian Outcaste: The Autobiography of an Untouchable* by Hazari—and the other discovered on a newsstand book rack at the Jersey shore—the autobiography of Leroy "Satchel" Paige, *Maybe I'll Pitch Forever*, a great favorite too of a young Philip Roth.

5   Shechner, *Up Society's Ass*, 172.

6   Shechner, *Up Society's Ass*.

7   Sandra Kumamoto Stanley, "Mourning the 'Greatest Generation': Myth and History in Philip Roth's *American Pastoral*," *Twentieth Century Literature* 51 (Spring, 2005): 1–24.

8 "Peaceful War Protest Ends Brookside Parade," *The Observer-Tribune*, July 10, 1969. Note: Ken Lurie graciously shared with me this article in *The Observer-Tribune*. The personal clipping and photocopy of the article he sent me contains the date of the article, but it is missing its page number. *The Observer-Tribune* has no copy of it on microfilm or digitized and neither does any library in Morris County. It must be endnoted as n.p.

18. *American Pastoral* and Revolutions of the Word

1 Roland Barthes, *Writing Degree Zero* (New York: Hill & Wang, 1953).

2 Oliver Wendell Holmes Sr., *The Professor at the Breakfast Table* (Boston: Houghton Mifflin, 1892), 41–42.

3 Thomas Paine, *The Crisis*, in *The Life and Major Writings of Thomas Paine*, ed. Philip S. Foner (Secaucus, NJ: The Citadel Press, 1948), 50.

4 Jefferson, *Writings*, 19–20.

5 In the last public letter of his life (a message to the *New Yorker* published in its January 30, 2017, issue), Roth advises: "Trump is just a con artist. The relevant book about Trump's American forebear is Herman Melville's '*The Confidence-Man*'" (Thurman, Judith. "Philip Roth's E-mails on Trump." *The New Yorker*, January 30, 2017, www.newyorker.com/magazine /2017/01/30/philip-roth-e-mails-on-trump).

6 See my own description of the political linguistics of the revolution in chapter 7 of *Representative Words*. For my take on the politics of language in Roth's *Human Stain* and the counterpoint in his writings between the office of the letter and the bomb, the word and violence, see my essay in *Philip Roth Studies* (Fall 2023) entitled "Athenian Logomachy in *The Human Stain* and Philip Roth's Fight for the Word."

7 Jefferson, *Writings*, 23.

Epilogue

1 Susanne Antonetta, "Elizabeth," in *Italian American Writers on New Jersey: An Anthology of Poetry and Prose,* ed. Jennifer Gillan, Maria Mazziotti Gillan, and Edvige Giunta (New Brunswick, NJ: Rutgers University Press, 2003), 280.

2 Angus Kress Gillespie and Michael Aaron Rockland, *Looking for America on the New Jersey Turnpike* (New Brunswick, NJ: Rutgers University Press, 1989). Paterson is the literary home of William Carlos Williams and Allen Ginsberg but also a key setting for Junot Diaz's *The Brief Wondrous Life of Oscar Wao* and two novels by John Updike: *In the Beauty of the Lilies* and *The Terrorist*.

3 Irina Reyn, ed., *Living on the Edge of the World: New Jersey Writers Take on the Garden State* (New York: Touchstone, 2007). Similarly, Joe Vallese and Alicia A. Beale have edited an anthology of New Jersey literature entitled *What's Your Exit: A Literary Detour through New Jersey* (Middletown, NJ: Word Riot Press, 2010) in which one version of its table of contents is organized by exit signs off the New Jersey Turnpike and the Garden State Parkway. Roth's *American Trilogy* has been called by one scholar the Newark Trilogy, but what is intriguing to note is that in both *The Human Stain* and *I Married a Communist* (as well as in *American Pastoral*) a small town in rural New Jersey unmarked by any exit off the Turnpike or Parkway has a not insignificant cameo role. It is Gouldtown in Cumberland County in *The Human Stain*, a place that has its origins in a controversial interracial marriage between a Black man named Gould and Elizabeth Fenwick, an Anglo woman who was the granddaughter of John Fenwick, a wealthy English colonist who emigrated to the region in 1675. An *Ebony Magazine* article in 1952 called Gouldtown "America's Oldest Negro Community" (February 1952, pp. 42–46). In *I Married a Communist*, Ira Ringold, as a young man, lives and works for over two years in Zinc Town located in the novel in northwestern New Jersey in Sussex County. Zinc Town is perhaps modeled on Ogdensburg and the Sterling Hill Mine. Here is where Ira first begins to develop his connection to working-class politics and communism. In *American Pastoral*, of course, Old Rimrock has a starring role. All three locations are obscure, but very representative in revealing ways about the history and character of unlimned sides of New Jersey. Strangely, James F. Broderick's anthology, *Paging New Jersey: A Literary Guide to the Garden State* (New Brunswick, NJ: Rutgers University Press, 2003), includes Roth's *Goodbye, Columbus* but leaves out mention of *American Pastoral*.

4   Robert Pinsky, *Jersey Breaks: Becoming an American Poet* (New York: Norton, 2022), 1.

5   Pinksy, *Jersey Breaks*.

6   One relatively unknown example of such a novel is William Carlos Williams's *The Build-Up* (New York: Random House, 1952), the third part of a trilogy that focuses on the life of the Stetchers, an immigrant family with a father from East Prussia and mother from Norway who settle in the lower working-class town of Hackensack, New Jersey. The father, Joe, begins a printing business that becomes a success, which enables the family to move to the much more upscale Riverdale, New Jersey, a small suburban community, where his wife, Gurlie, becomes very active in becoming a "success" in the higher social circles of the town.

7   For lyrics to "Goodbye, Columbus" (1969) by The Association, which was part of the soundtrack for the film version of "Goodbye, Columbus" (1969), see https://www.azlyrics.com /lyrics/association/goodbyecolumbus.html.

8   Cohen, *A Consumers' Republic*, 197.

9   Cohen, *A Consumers' Republic*.

10 This study is obviously caught in an ambivalence. On the one hand, I see Brookside as Swede embraces Old Rimrock—and as my parents embraced it—as a holy land akin to the way D. J. Waldie approaches Lakewood, California in his extraordinary memoir and history, *Holy Land: A Suburban Memoir* (New York: Norton, 1996). On the other hand, I also approach it closer to the spirit of two other Levovs—Jerry and Merry—in their irreverence and anger at this place as an "unholy land." For a cultural history of attitudes toward the suburbs in American literature, see Catherine Jurca's *White Diaspora: The Suburb and the Twentieth Century American Novel* (Princeton, NJ: Princeton University Press, 2001). Complementing this leading foray in literary criticism of the suburb are a set of cultural and historical studies of the suburban and small-town world in America, with my favorite being Miles Orvell's *The Death and Life of Main Street: Small Towns in American Memory, Space, and Community* (Chapel Hill: University of North Carolina Press, 2012). Another study of small towns in America, in the vein of memoir and cultural study, is Robert Pinsky's *Thousands of Broadways: Dreams and Nightmares of the American Small Town* (Chicago: University

of Chicago Press, 2009), with his hometown of Long Branch at the center of his reflections. (He updates and extends this story in *Jersey Breaks*.) See also Ryan Poll, *Main Street and Empire: The Fictional Small Town in the Age of Globalization* (New Brunswick, NJ: Rutgers University Press, 2012) for a study about how the small town has been figured in American culture and politics to represent the nation to the point that it becomes, in terms so fittingly appropriate to describe Swede's vision of Old Rimrock and Brookside's vision of itself, an island of U.S. exceptionalism.

11 Andrew Delbanco, *The Puritan Ordeal* (Cambridge, MA: Harvard University Press, 1991).

12 Grace Cavalieri, "Trenton," in *Italian American Writers on New Jersey: An Anthology of Poetry and Prose*, ed. Jennifer Gillan, Maria Mazziotti Gillan, and Edvige Giunta (New Brunswick, NJ: Rutgers University Press, 2003), 40.

13 Norman Mailer, "Superman Comes to the Supermarket," in *The Time of Our Time* (New York: Modern Library, 1999), 347.

14 Roth quoted in Paul Gray, "Novelist: Philip Roth."

15 For a photographic history of this estate world and the wealth along Madison Avenue from Madison to Mendham Township, see John W. Rae, *Mansions of Morris County* (Charleston, SC: Arcadia Publishing, 1999), especially chapter 1, "Madison Avenue: The Great White Way Country."

16 My own high school alma mater, The Pingry School, is another example of this exodus. Founded in 1861 and originally located in the Elizabeth-Hillside area, where I attended it from 1967 to 1971, it moved to Martinsville, New Jersey in Somerset County on a 192-acre campus. In 2021, it purchased the grounds and buildings of The Purnell School on 82 acres in the rolling hills of Pottersville, New Jersey as an additional campus.

17 Dennis E. Gale in *Greater New Jersey: Living in the Shadow of Gotham* (Philadelphia: University of Pennsylvania Press, 2006) takes us on an illuminating descriptive journey from Morristown to Penn Station along the rail lines of the Erie Lackawanna in the prologue aptly entitled "Into the Belly of the Beast," 1–11.

18 Cited from the History section of Picatinny Arsenal website: https://home.army.mil/picatinny/.

19 See Ard and Rockland, "Anti-Semitism: The Snake in the Garden State," chapter 9 in *The Jews of New Jersey: A Pictorial History*, 104–110.

20 Hummel, *A Journey through Literary America*, 243–244.

21 J. Hector St. John de Crèvecoeur, *Letters from an American Farmer and Sketches of Eighteenth-Century America* (New York: Penguin Classics, 1981), letter 3, 66–67.

22 Antonetta, "Elizabeth," 276.

23 Claudia Roth Pierpont, *Roth: A Writer and His Books* (New York: Farrar, Straus & Giroux, 2013), 322.

24 Williams, *Paterson*, n.p. Allen Ginsberg, "Garden State," in *Collected Poems 1947–1997* (New York: Harper, 2007), 726.

25 Williams, *Paterson*, n.p.

26 I would add that what makes Jim Jarmusch's *Paterson* (2016) such a beautiful, resonant film are the qualities that Roth embraces for his own fiction: a passion for specificity—the particulars of the history of a place—and for the poetry of a place: its feel, its imagery, and the metaphors of its facts. This is literally the case of *Paterson*, which draws on the history of its local legends associated with Paterson from sports and film and politics as well as literature that the barkeeper in the film, Doc, gives homage to in his bar: Gaetano Bresci (anarchist), Rubin "Hurricane" Carter (boxer), Lou Costello (comedian), Larry Doby (the second African American to break into Major League Baseball), Allen Ginsberg (poet), Bruce Vilanch (Oscar-winning writer), and William Carlos Williams (poet).

Bibliography

"America's Most Expensive Zip Codes." *Forbes Magazine*, August 27, 2009. https://www.forbes.com/2009/08/26/most -expensive-zip-codes-lifestyle-real-estate-zips_slide.html.

Antonetta, Susanne. "Elizabeth." In *Italian American Writers on New Jersey: An Anthology of Poetry and Prose*, edited by Jennifer Gillan, Maria Mazziotti Gillan, and Edvige Giunta, 270–281. New Brunswick, NJ: Rutgers University Press, 2003.

Ard, Patricia, and Michael Aaron Rockland. *The Jews of New Jersey: A Pictorial History*. New Brunswick, NJ: Rutgers University Press, 2002.

"The Association Lyrics: 'Goodbye, Columbus.'" AZ. Accessed December 10, 2023. https://www.azlyrics.com/lyrics /association/goodbyecolumbus.html.

Axtell, S. B. "Mendham Township." In *The History of Morris County, New Jersey, with Illustrations and Biographical Sketches of Prominent Citizens and Pioneers*. New York: W. W. Munsell & Co., 1882.

Auden, W. H. *Secondary Worlds*. New York: Random House, 1968.

Bailey, Blake. *Philip Roth: The Biography*. New York: Norton, 2021.

Barthes, Roland. *Writing Degree Zero*. New York: Hill & Wang, 1953.

Bercovitch, Sacvan. *American Jeremiad*. Madison: University of Wisconsin Press, 1978.

Broderick, James F. *Paging New Jersey: A Literary Guide to the Garden State*. New Brunswick, NJ: Rutgers University Press, 2003.

Bureau, Claire Heininger/Statehouse. "GOP Candidate Chris Christie Launched Political Career as Morris County

Freeholder." NJ. May 12, 2009. https://www.nj.com/news
/2009/05/gop_candidate_chris_christie_1.html.

Cavalieri, Grace. "Trenton." In *Italian American Writers on New
Jersey: An Anthology of Poetry and Prose*, edited by Jennifer
Gillan, Maria Mazziotti Gillan, and Edvige Giunta, 39–40.
New Brunswick, NJ: Rutgers University Press, 2003.

Census Reporter. Brookside, New Jersey. Accessed December 10,
2023. https://censusreporter.org/profiles/16000US3408260
-brookside-nj/.

Census Reporter. Mendham Township, New Jersey. Accessed
December 10, 2023. https://censusreporter.org/profiles
/06000US3402745360-mendham-township-morris-county-nj/.

Cohen, Lizabeth. *A Consumers' Republic: The Politics of Mass
Consumption in Postwar America*. New York: Vintage, 2004.

Coughlin, Kevin. "Remembering One of Morristown's Finest:
George Jenkins Sr., a Community Cop for Turbulent Times |
Morristown Green." January 10, 2017. Accessed December 10,
2023. https://morristowngreen.com/2017/01/10/remembering
-one-of-morristowns-finest-george-jenkins-sr-a-community
-cop-for-turbulent-times/.

Cramer, Steven. *Goodbye to the Orchard*. Louisville, KY: Sarabande Books, 2004.

———. *The World Book*. Providence, RI: Copper Beech Press, 1992.

Crèvecoeur, J. Hector St. John de. *Letters from an American
Farmer and Sketches of Eighteenth-Century America*. New
York: Penguin Classics, 1981.

Cunningham, John T. "Mendham: My Home." *Crossroads
Magazine*, November 1965. In Mendham Borough Library
archives.

———. *This Is New Jersey*. 4th ed. New Brunswick, NJ: Rutgers
University Press, 2001.

———. *The Uncertain Revolution: Washington & the Continental
Army at Morristown*. West Creek, NJ: Cormorant Publishing,
2007.

Day, Colleen. "Newark before the Comeback: A City Marked by
White Flight, Poor Policy," *NJ Spotlight News,* September 9,
2019. https://www.njspotlightnews.org/2019/09/19-09-02
-newark-before-the-comeback-a-city-marked-by-white-flight
-and-poor-policy/.

"The Decline of Randolphs Great Resorts." New Jersey Hills.
October 13, 2005. https://www.newjerseyhills.com/the-decline

-of-randolph-s-great- resorts/article_0ce51d5e-ac25-5c2c-a1b8
-84c21e234510.html.

Delbanco, Andrew. *The Puritan Ordeal*. Cambridge, MA:
    Harvard University Press, 1991.

Department of the Interior. National Register of Historic Places
    Registration Form for Brookside. 1996. https://npgallery.nps
    .gov/GetAsset/78d1e543-4bb2-4b7a-8870-40b7fa96bdb4.

Ellison, Ralph. *Going to the Territory*. New York: Random House,
    1986.

———. *Shadow and Act*. New York: New American Library,
    1966.

Emerson, Ralph Waldo. *Essays and Lectures*. New York: Library of
    America, 1983.

Fitzgerald, Frances. *Fire in the Lake*. Boston: Little, Brown, 1972.

Fitzgerald, F. Scott. *The Great Gatsby*. New York: Scribner's Sons,
    1925.

Forgosh, Linda B. *Jews of Morris County*. Charleston, SC: Arcadia
    Press, 2006.

Gale, Dennis E. *Greater New Jersey: Living in the Shadow of
    Gotham*. Philadelphia: University of Pennsylvania Press, 2006.

Garber, Phil. "It's Back to the 60's for Brookside July 4 Parade."
    Observer-Tribune News, New Jersey Hills, June 18, 2012.
    https://www.newjerseyhills.com/observer-tribune/news/it-s
    -back-to-the-60s-for-brookside-july-4-parade/article_1dc26b88
    -b976-11e1-8d7a- 001a4bcf887a.html.

Gillespie, Angus Kress, and Michael Aaron Rockland. *Looking for
    America on the New Jersey Turnpike*. New Brunswick, NJ:
    Rutgers University Press, 1989.

Gillette, Howard, Jr. "Suburbanization and the Decline of the
    Cities: Toward an Uncertain Future." In *New Jersey: A History of
    the Garden State*, edited by Maxine N. Lurie and Richard Veit,
    264–285. New Brunswick, NJ: Rutgers University Press, 2012.

Ginsberg, Allen. *Collected Poems 1947–1997*. New York: Harper,
    2007.

"The Grandest Little Hometown Parade in America Wants You!"
    Mendham Township, New Jersey. Accessed November 24,
    2023. https://www.mendhamtownship.org/home/news
    /grandest-little-hometown-parade-america-wants-you.

Gray, Paul. "Novelist: Philip Roth." *Time Magazine*, July 9, 2001.
    https://content.time.com/time/subscriber/article
    /0,33009,1000283,00.html.

Gray, Thomas, *Elegy Written in a Country Churchyard*. Mount Vernon, New York: Peter Pauper Press, 1947.

Green, Howard L. *Words that Make New Jersey History: A Primary Source Reader*. New Brunswick, NJ: Rutgers University Press, 2009.

Gustafson, Thomas. *Representative Words: Politics, Literature, and the American Language 1776–1865*. Cambridge: Cambridge University Press, 1992.

Halio, Jay L., and Ben Siegel. *Turning Up the Flame: Philip Roth's Later Novels*. Newark: University of Delaware Press, 2005.

Hawthorne, Nathaniel. *Nathaniel Hawthorne; Tales and Sketches*. New York: Library of America, 1982.

Hazelgrove, William. *Morristown: The Darkest Winter of the Revolutionary War and the Plot to Kidnap George Washington*. Guilford, CT: Lyons Press, 2021.

Heininger, Claire. "GOP Candidate Chris Christie Launched Political Career as Morris County Freeholder," May 12, 2009. https://www.nj.com/news/2009/05/gop_candidate_chris _christie_l.html.

Holmes, Oliver Wendell, Sr. *The Professor at the Breakfast Table*. Boston: Houghton Mifflin, 1892.

Hopler, Martha G., Edward W. Roseller, and Wallace G. West. *The Mendhams*. Mayor's Tercentenary Committee, The Township Committee of the Township of Mendham, 1964.

Hummel, Thomas R. *A Journey through Literary America*. Napa, CA: Val De Grace Books, 2009.

Ingle, Bob, and Michael Symons. *Chris Christie: The Inside Story of His Rise to Power*. New York: St. Martin's Press, 2012.

Jefferson, Thomas. *Writings*. New York: Library of America, 1984.

"Jenkins v. Tp. Of Morris School Dist. And Bd. Of Ed." Justia Law. Accessed November 24, 2023. https://law.justia.com /cases/new-jersey/supreme-court/1971/58-n-j-483-0.html.

Johnson, Dana. *In the Not Quite Dark: Stories*. Berkeley, CA: Counterpoint, 2016.

Jurca, Catherine. *White Diaspora: The Suburb and the Twentieth-Century American Novel*. Princeton, NJ: Princeton University Press, 2001.

Kaplan, Brett Ashley. *Jewish Anxiety in the Novels of Philip Roth*. London: Bloomsbury Academic, 2016.

Kausch, Katie. "Mendham's Annual 4th of July Parade In Brookside Back for 2019," *The Patch,* June 21, 2019. Accessed December 10, 2023. https://patch.com/new-jersey/mendham -chester/mendhams-annual-4th-july-parade-brookside-back -2019.

Kimmage, Michael. *In History's Grip: Philip Roth's Newark Trilogy.* Stanford, CA: Stanford University Press, 2012.

King, Martin Luther, Jr. *A Testament of Hope: The Essential Writings and Speeches.* New York: Harper, 2003.

Kominsky, Karen. "The Rise and Decline of Resorts in Mt. Freedom." *New Jersey Hills*, October 13, 2005.

Kushner, Tony. *Thinking about the Longstanding Problem of Virtue: Essays, a Play, Two Poems, and a Prayer.* Theater Communications Group, 1995.

Lepore, Jill. "Battleground America: One Nation, Under the Gun." *New Yorker*, April 23, 2012.

Limerick, Patricia. *The Legacy of Conquest: The Unbroken Past of the American West.* New York: Norton, 1987.

Lowell, James Russell. *The Works of James Russell Lowell.* 10 vols. Boston: Houghton Mifflin, 1890.

Lurie, Maxine N. *Taking Sides in Revolutionary New Jersey.* New Brunswick, NJ: Rutgers University Press, 2022.

"Madison Divided on Barber Ruling; Order to Cut Negroes' Hair Is Hailed and Criticized." *New York Times*, December 18, 1964, sec. Archives. https://www.nytimes.com/1964/12/18/archives /madison-divided-on-barber-ruling-order-to-cut-negroes-hair -is.html.

Madison, James. *Notes of Debates in the Federal Convention of 1787 Reported by James Madison.* Edited by Adrienne Koch. New York: Norton, 1969.

Mailer, Norman. *The Time of Our Time.* New York: Modern Library, 1999.

Mancall, Peter C. *The Trials of Thomas Morton: An Anglican Lawyer, His Puritan Foes, and the Battle for New England.* New Haven, CT: Yale University Press, 2019.

Masiero, Pia. *Philip Roth and the Zuckerman Books: The Making of a Storyworld.* Amherst, NY: Cambria Press, 2011.

Melville, Herman. *Billy Budd, Sailor.* Edited by Harrison Hayford and Merton M. Sealts, Jr. Chicago: University of Chicago Press, 1962.

———. *Melville.* New York: Library of America, 1984.

"Mendham Golf and Tennis Club | Private Club Mendham NJ."
Accessed November 24, 2023. https://www
.mendhamgolfandtennis.com.

Mendham Township. Accessed December 7, 2023. http://www
.mendhamtownship.org.

Mendham Township Historic Preservation Committee. Accessed
December 7, 2023. http://www.historicmendhamtwp.com.

Mendham Township School District. Historical Overview.
Accessed December 10, 2023. https://www.mendhamtwp.org
/community.

Merrill, Christopher. "Dismal Harmony." *Third Coast*, Fall 2005.

———. *Self-Portrait with Dogwood*. San Antonio: Trinity
University Press, 2017.

———. *Workbook*. Santa Fe: Teal Press, 1988.

Meyer, Michael M., ed. *Joachim Prinz, Rebellious Rabbi*. Bloomington: Indiana University Press, 2008.

"In Morris, a Painful Schools Merger." *New York Times*, October 21, 1973, sec. Archives. https://www.nytimes.com/1973/10
/21/archives/in-morris-a-painful-schools-merger-merger-in
-morris-is-proving.html.

"Morris County, NJ | Data USA." Datausa. Accessed Novem-
ber 24, 2023. https://datausa.io/profile/geo/morris-county
-nj#:~:text=The%205%20largest%20ethnic%20groups.

Morris County. New Jersey Website. Accessed December 10, 2023.
https://www.morriscountynj.gov/Home.

Morrison, Toni. *The Nobel Lecture in Literature*. New York:
Knopf, 1993.

"Newark." Wikipedia. April 13, 2023. http://en.wikipedia.org
/wiki/Newark.

Ortner, Sherry B. *New Jersey Dreaming: Capital, Culture, and the
Class of 1958*. Durham, NC: Duke University Press, 2003.

Orvell, Miles. *The Death and Life of Main Street: Small Towns in
American Memory, Space, and Community*. Chapel Hill:
University of North Carolina Press, 2012.

Paine, Thomas. *The Crisis, in The Life and Major Writings of
Thomas Paine*. Edited by Philip S. Foner. Secaucus: The Citadel
Press, 1948.

"Peaceful War Protest Ends Brookside Parade." *The Observer-
Tribune*. July 10, 1969.

Philip Roth at 80: A Celebration. New York: Library of America,
2014.

"Philip Roth (RIP) Creates a List of the 15 Books That Influenced Him Most." Open Culture. Accessed November 24, 2023. https://www.openculture.com/2018/05/philip-roth-rip-creates-a-list-of-the-15-books-that-influenced-him-most.html.

Picatinny Arsenal website. Accessed December 10, 2023. https://home.army.mil/picatinny/about/history.

Pierpont, Claudia Roth. *Roth: A Writer and His Books*. New York: Farrar, Straus & Giroux, 2013.

Pinsky, Robert. *Jersey Breaks: Becoming an American Poet*. New York: Norton. 2022.

———. *Thousands of Broadways: Dreams and Nightmares of the American Small Town*. Chicago: University of Chicago Press, 2009.

Poll, Ryan. *Main Street and Empire: The Fictional Small Town in the Age of Globalization*. New Brunswick, NJ: Rutgers University Press, 2012.

Pozorski, Aimee. *Roth and Trauma: The Problem of History in the Later Works (1995–2010)*. New York: Continuum, 2011.

Prevost, Lisa. *Snob Zones: Fear, Prejudice and Real Estate*. Boston: Beacon Press, 2013.

Pynchon, Thomas. *The Crying of Lot 49*. New York: Harper, 1966.

Rae, John W. *Mansions of Morris County*. Charleston, SC: Arcadia Publishing, 1999.

Reagan, Ronald. "Second Inaugural Address." 1985. https://avalon.law.yale.edu/20th_century/reagan2.asp.

Reilly, Donald, "Religious Freedom Is My Immediate Goal." *New Yorker*, June 3, 1974. https://condenaststore.com/featured/religious-freedom-is-my-immediate-goal-donald-reilly.html.

Reyn, Irina, ed. *Living on the Edge of the World: New Jersey Writers Take on the Garden State*. New York: Touchstone, 2007.

Robinson, P. C. "Taking Pride in Brookside." New Jersey Hills. July 1, 2022. https://www.newjerseyhills.com/observer-tribune/news/taking-pride-in-brookside/image_ccefd64f-a27e-547b-a50a-bfbb3e847e12.html.

Rodriguez, Robyn Magalit. *In Lady Liberty's Shadow: The Politics of Race and Immigration in New Jersey*. New Brunswick, NJ: Rutgers University Press, 2017.

Rosenthal, Michael. *The Character Factory: Baden-Powell and the Origins of the Boy Scout Movement*. New York: Pantheon, 1986.

Roth, Philip. *American Pastoral*. Boston: Houghton, 1997.

——. *The Counterlife*. New York: Vintage, 1996.

——. *The Dying Animal*. New York: Vintage, 2001.

——. *I Married a Communist*. New York: Vintage, 1999.

——. *Reading Myself and Others*. New York: Vintage, 2001.

Rowe, John Carlos. *Afterlives of Modernism: Liberalism, Transnationalism, and Political Critique*. Hanover, NH: Dartmouth College Press, 2011.

Shechner, Mark. "Roth's American Trilogy." In *The Cambridge Companion to Philip Roth*, edited by Timothy Parrish, 142–157. Cambridge: Cambridge University Press, 2007.

——. *Up Society's Ass, Copper: Rereading Philip Roth*. Madison: University of Wisconsin Press, 2003.

Shostak, Deborah, ed. *Philip Roth: American Pastoral, The Human Stain, The Plot Against America*. London: Continuum, 2011.

Slotkin, Richard. *The Fatal Environment: The Myth of the Frontier in the Age of Industrialization, 1800–1890*. New York: Macmillan, 1985.

——. *Gunfighter Nation: Myth of the Frontier in Twentieth Century*. New York: Atheneum, 1992.

——. *Regeneration through Violence: The Mythology of the American Frontier, 1600–1800*. Middletown, CT: Wesleyan University Press, 1974.

Stanley, Sandra Kumamoto. "Mourning the 'Greatest Generation': Myth and History in Philip Roth's *American Pastoral*." *Twentieth Century Literature* 51 (Spring 2005): 1–24.

Stockton, Frank R. *Stories of New Jersey*. New Brunswick, NJ: Rutgers University Press, 1961.

Sullivan, Ronald. "War Protestors Meet Opposition." *New York Times*, September 6, 1970.

Thurman, Judith. "Philip Roth's E-mails on Trump." *The New Yorker*, January 2017. https://www.newyorker.com/magazine/2017/01/30/philip-roth-e-mails-on-trump.

"The Ties That Bind: How Relations Shaped Morris County and New Jersey, 1688–2018." Morris Museum. Accessed November 24, 2023. https://morrismuseum.org/on-view/past-exhibitions/the-ties-that-bind#:~:text=Organized%20by%20Bethel%20Church%20of.

Twain, Mark. *The Adventures of Huckleberry Finn*. New York: Penguin, 2003.

U.S. Census Bureau, Mendham Township. Accessed December 10, 2022. https://www.census.gov/quickfacts/mendhamto
wnshipmorriscountynewjersey.

Vallese, Joe, and Alicia A. Beale, eds. *What's Your Exit? A Literary Detour through New Jersey*. Middletown, NJ: Word Riot Press, 2010.

Waldie, D. J. *Holy Land: A Suburban Memoir*. New York: Norton, 1996.

Wilentz, Sean. "An Acute Sense of History." In *Philip Roth Personal Library*. Newark, NJ: Newark Public Library, 2022.

Williams, William Carlos. *The Build-Up*. New York: Random House, 1952.

———. *Paterson*. New York: New Directions, 1963.

Wright, Boyd. *Jockey Hollow: A Novel of the American Revolution*. Bloomington, IN: 1st Books Library, 2003.

Index

Note: Page numbers in italics refer to figures.

About the Author

THOMAS GUSTAFSON is an associate professor of English at the University of Southern California. He is the author of *Representative Words: Politics, Literature, and the American Language, 1776–1865*. Born and raised in Brookside, New Jersey, he now calls Echo Park in Los Angeles his home.

Available titles in the Ceres: Rutgers Studies in History series: